THE LIBRARY OF
CHRISTMAS
FAVOURITES

GW00672140

COMPILED BY AMY APPLEBY AND PETER PICKOW
SPECIAL THANKS TO JACQUELINE TORRANCE FOR EDITORIAL ASSISTANCE

ORDER NO. AM 948850
US INTERNATIONAL STANDARD BOOK NUMBER: 0.8256.1704.9
UK INTERNATIONAL STANDARD BOOK NUMBER: 0.7119.7584.1

EXCLUSIVE DISTRIBUTORS:
MUSIC SALES CORPORATION
257 PARK AVENUE SOUTH, NEW YORK, NY 10010 USA
MUSIC SALES LIMITED
8/9 FRITH STREET, LONDON W1V 5TZ ENGLAND
MUSIC SALES PTY. LIMITED
120 ROTHSCHILD STREET, ROSEBERY, SYDNEY, NSW 2018, AUSTRALIA

PRINTED IN THE UNITED STATES OF AMERICA BY
VICKS LITHOGRAPH AND PRINTING CORPORATION

AMSCO PUBLICATIONS
NEW YORK/LONDON/PARIS/SYDNEY

Christmas Songs and Carols

THE NIGHT BEFORE CHRISTMAS

ANGELS AND SHEPHERDS

THE LOWLY MANGER

Christmas Songs and Carols

MARY AND JOSEPH

WE THREE KINGS

COME LET US ADORE HIM

GLAD TIDINGS FOR CHRISTMAS

Christmas Songs and Carols

Christmas Classics

Christmas Songs and Carols

Silent Night

Words by Joseph Mohr
(1792–1849)

Music by Franz Xaver Gruber
(1787–1863)

2. Silent night! Holy night!
Shepherds quake at the sight!
Glories stream from heaven afar,
Heav'nly hosts sing Alleluia,
Christ, the Savior, is born!
Christ, the Savior, is born!

3. Silent night! Holy night!
Sun of God, love's pure light,
Radiant beams from Thy holy face,
With the dawn of redeeming grace,
Jesus, Lord at Thy birth,
Jesus, Lord at Thy birth.

4. Silent night! Holy night!
Wondrous star, lend thy light;
With the angels let us sing
Alleluia to our King;
Christ, the Savior is born.
Christ, the Savior is born.

The Moon Shines Bright

Traditional English carol

1. The moon shines bright and the stars give light, A
2. A-wake, a-wake, good peo-ple all, A-

lit-tle be-fore the day; Our mighty Lord, He
wake, and you shall hear, The Lord our God He died

looked on us, And bade us a-wake and pray!
on the cross, For us He loved so dear.

It Came Upon a Midnight Clear

(first version)

Words by Edmund Hamilton Sears
(1810–1876)

Music by Richard Storrs Willis
(1819–1900)

2. Still through the cloven skies they come,
   With peaceful wings unfurled,
   And still their heav'nly music floats
   O'er all the weary world;
   Above its sad and lowly plain
   They bend on hovering wing,
   And ever over its Babel sounds
   The blessèd angels sing.

3. Yet with the woes of sin and strife
   The world has suffered long;
   Beneath the angel-strain have rolled
   Two thousand years of wrong;
   And man, at war with man, hears not
   The love-song which they bring.
   O hush the noise, ye men of strife,
   And hear the angels sing.

4. And ye, beneath life's crushing load,
   Whose forms are bending low,
   Who toil along the climbing way
   With weary steps and slow:
   Look up! for glad and golden hours
   Come swiftly on the wing;
   O rest beside the weary road
   And hear the angels sing.

5. For lo! the days are hastening on,
   By prophet bards foretold,
   When with the ever-circling years
   Comes round the Age of Gold.
   When peace shall over all the earth
   Its ancient splendors fling,
   And the whole world give back the song
   Which now the angels sing.

It Came Upon a Midnight Clear
(second version)

Words by Edmund Hamilton Sears
(1810–1876)

Traditional English air

heav'n's e - ter - nal king. The world in sol - emn___
bend on hov - 'ring wing. And e - ver o'er its___

still - ness lay, to ___ hear ___ the an - gels sing.
Ba - bel sounds the ___ bles - sed an - gels sing.

3. Yet with the woes of sin and strife
   The world has suffered long;
   Beneath the angel-strain have rolled
   Two thousand years of wrong;
   And man, at war with man, hears not
   The love-song which they bring.
   O hush the noise, ye men of strife,
   And hear the angels sing.

4. And ye, beneath life's crushing load,
   Whose forms are bending low,
   Who toil along the climbing way
   With weary steps and slow:
   Look up! for glad and golden hours
   Come swiftly on the wing;
   O rest beside the weary road
   And hear the angels sing.

5. For lo! the days are hastening on,
   By prophet bards foretold,
   When with the ever-circling years
   Comes round the Age of Gold.
   When peace shall over all the earth
   Its ancient splendors fling,
   And the whole world give back the song
   Which now the angels sing.

O Little Town of Bethlehem

(first version)

Words by Phillips Brooks
(1835–1893)

Music by Lewis H. Redner
(1831–1908)

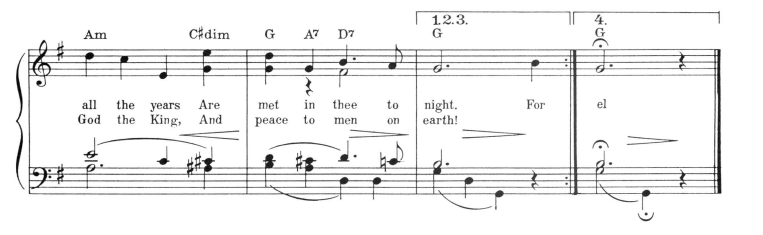

all the years Are met in thee to night. For el
God the King, And peace to men on earth!

3. How silently, how silently,
   The wondrous gift is giv'n!
   So God imparts to human hearts
   The blessing of His heav'n.
   No ear may hear His coming,
   But in this world of sin,
   Where meek souls will receive Him still
   The dear Christ enters in.

4. O Holy Child of Bethlehem!
   Descend to us, we pray;
   Cast out our sin, and enter in;
   Be born in us today.
   We hear the Christmas angels
   The great glad tidings tell;
   O come to us, abide with us,
   Our Lord Emmanuel.

O Little Town of Bethlehem
(second version)

Words by Phillips Brooks
(1835–1893)

Traditional English ballad

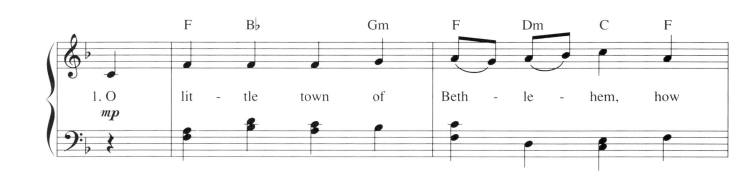

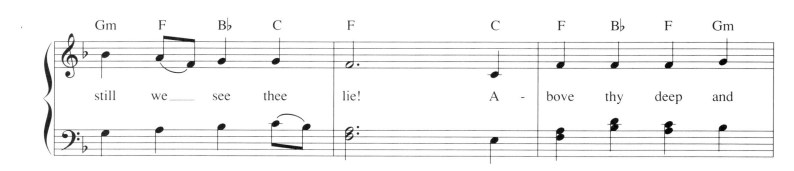

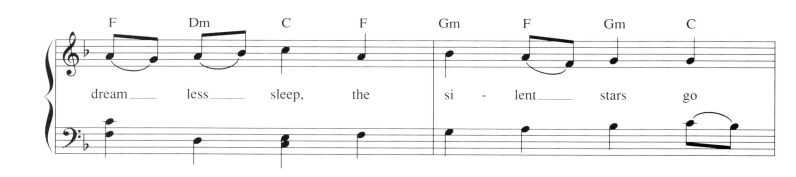

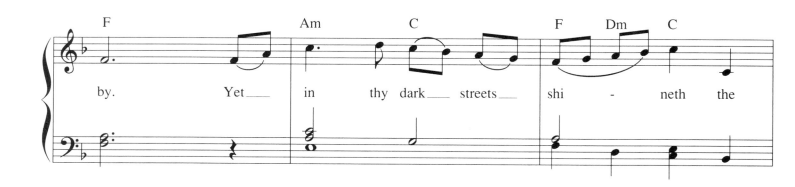

ev - er - last - ing light. The hopes and fears of

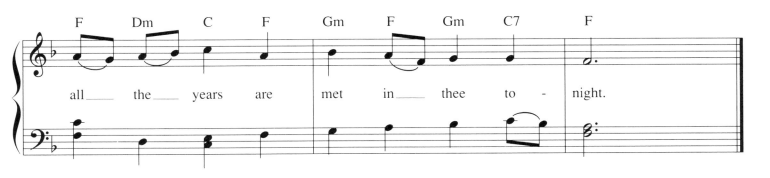

all___ the___ years are met in___ thee to - night.

2. For Christ is born of Mary
   And gathered all above
   While mortals sleep, the angels keep
   Their watch of wond'ring love.
   O morning stars, together
   Proclaim Thy holy birth!
   And praises sing to God the King
   And peace to men on earth.

3. How silently, how silently,
   The wondrous gift is giv'n!
   So God imparts to human hearts
   The blessing of His heav'n.
   No ear may hear His coming,
   But in this world of sin,
   Where meek souls will receive Him still
   The dear Christ enters in.

4. O Holy Child of Bethlehem!
   Descend to us, we pray;
   Cast out our sin, and enter in;
   Be born in us today.
   We hear the Christmas angels
   The great glad tidings tell;
   O come to us, abide with us,
   Our Lord Emmanuel.

All My Heart This Night Rejoices

Words by Paul Gerhardt
(1607–1676)

Music by Johann G. Ebeling
(1637–1676)

2. Hark! a voice from yonder manger
   Soft and sweet, doth entreat;
   "Flee from woe and danger;
   Brethren come; from all that grieves you
   You are freed; all you need
   I will surely give you."

3. Come, then, let us hasten yonder;
   Here let all, great and small
   Kneel in awe and wonder;
   Love Him, who with love is yearning;
   Hail the star, that from far
   Bright with hope is burning!

O Holy Night!

English words by John Sullivan Dwight

Music by Adolphe Adam
(1803–1856)

All Through the Night

Traditional Welsh carol

Past Three O'Clock

Traditional English carol

2. Seraph quire singeth,
Angel bell ringeth:
Hark how they rime it,
Time it, and chime it.
Refrain

3. Cheese from the dairy
Bring they for Mary,
And, not for money,
Butter and honey.
Refrain

4. Myrrh from full coffer,
Incense they offer:
Nor is the golden
Nugget witholden.
Refrain

5. Thus they: I pray you,
Up sirs, nor stay you
Till ye confess Him
Likewise, and bless Him.
Refrain

'Twas the Night Before Christmas

Words by Clement Clarke Moore
(1779–1863)

Traditional melody

ma in her 'ker - chief, and I in my cap, had just set - tled our brains for a

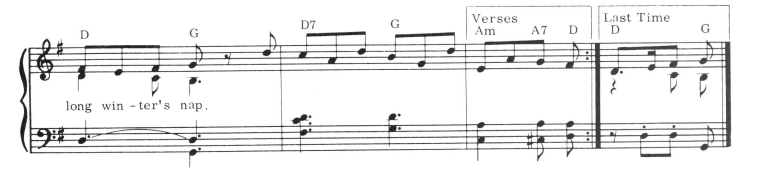

long win - ter's nap.

2. When out on the lawn there arose such a clatter,
I sprang from my bed to see what was the matter.
Away to the window I flew like a flash,
Tore open the shutters and threw up the sash.
The moon on the breast of the new-fallen snow,
Gave a luster of midday to objects below,
When, what to my wondering eyes should appear,
But a miniature sleigh, and eight tiny reindeer;

3. With a little old driver, so lively and quick,
I knew in a moment it must be St. Nick.
More rapid than eagles his coursers they came,
And he whistled, and shouted, and called them by name;
"Now, Dasher! now, Dancer! now, Prancer and Vixen!
On, Comet! on, Cupid! on Donner and Blitzen!
To the top of the porch, to the top of the wall!
Now, dash away, dash away, dash away all!"

4. As dry leaves that before the wild hurricane fly,
When they meet with an obstacle, mount to the sky
So up to the housetop the coursers they flew,
With the sleigh full of toys, and St. Nicholas, too.
And then in a twinkling, I heard on the roof
The prancing and pawing of each little hoof.
As I drew in my head, and was turning around,
Down the chimney St. Nicholas came with a bound.

5. He was dressed all in fur from his head to his foot,
And his clothes were all tarnished with ashes and soot,
A bundle of toys he had flung on his back,
And he looked like a peddlar just opening his pack.
His eyes how they twinkled! his dimples how merry!
His cheeks were like roses, his nose like a cherry,
His droll little mouth was drawn up like a bow,
And the beard of his chin was as white as the snow.

6. The stump of a pipe he held tight in his teeth,
And the smoke, it encircled his head like a wreath.
He had a broad face and a round little belly
That shook when he laughed, like a bowl full of jelly.
He was chubby and plump, a right jolly old elf,
And I laughed when I saw him, in spite of myself.
A wink of his eye, and a twist of his head,
Soon gave me to know I had nothing to dread.

7. He spoke not a word, but went straight to his work,
And filled all the stockings; then turned with a jerk,
And laying his finger aside of his nose,
And giving a nod, up the chimney he rose.
He sprang to his sleigh, to his team gave a whistle,
And away they all flew like the down of a thistle;
But I heard him exclaim, ere he drove out of sight,
"Happy Christmas to all, and to all a Good-night!"

Jolly Old St. Nicholas

Traditional Christmas song

2. When the clock is striking twelve,
   When I'm fast asleep,
   Down the chimney broad and black,
   With your pack you'll creep;
   All the stockings you will find
   Hanging in a row;
   Mine will be the shortest one,
   You'll be sure to know.

3. Johnny wants a pair of skates;
   Susy wants a dolly;
   Nelly wants a storybook;
   She thinks dolls are folly;
   As for me, my little brain
   Isn't very bright;
   Choose for me, old Santa Claus,
   What you think is right.

Up on the Housetop

Words and music by B.R. Hanby

2. First comes the stocking of little Nell;
   Oh, dear Santa, fill it well;
   Give her a dolly that laughs and cries,
   One that will open and shut her eyes.
   Refrain

3. Next comes the stocking of little Will;
   Oh, just see what a glorious fill;
   Here is a hammer and lots of tacks,
   Also a ball and a whip that cracks.
   Refrain

The First Nowell

Traditional English carol

Refrain

Now - ell, _____ Now - ell, Now - ell, Now - ell, _____

Born is the King _____ of Is - ra - el.

3. And by the light of that same star
   Three wise men came from country far;
   To seek for a king was their intent
   And to follow the star wheresoever it went:
   Refrain

4. This star drew nigh to the northwest;
   O'er Bethlehem it took its rest.
   And there it did both stop and stay
   Right over the place where Jesus lay.
   Refrain

5. Then entered in those wise men three
   Fell reverently upon their knee,
   And offered there in His presence
   Both gold and myrrh and frankincense.
   Refrain

6. Then let us all with one accord
   Sing praises to our heavenly Lord
   That hath made heaven and earth of naught
   And with His blood mankind hath brought.
   Refrain

Angels We Have Heard on High

Traditional French carol

3. Come to Bethlehem and see
   Him whose birth the angels sing;
   Come adore on bended knee
   Christ, the Lord, the newborn King.
     Refrain

4. See Him in a manger laid,
   Whom the choir of angels priase;
   Holy Spirit lend thine aid,
   While our hearts in love we raise.
     Refrain

Hark! the Herald Angels Sing

Words by Charles Wesley
(1707–1788)

Music by Felix Mendelssohn
(1809–1847)

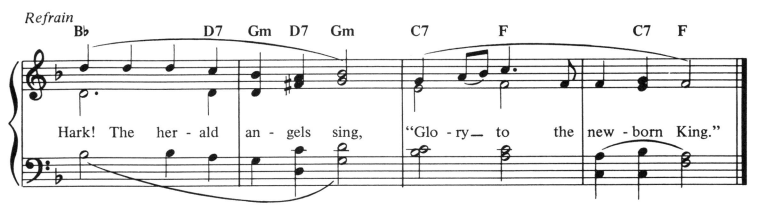

Refrain

Hark! The her-ald an-gels sing, "Glo-ry— to the new-born King."

2. Christ, by highest heaven adored;
Christ, the everlasting Lord;
Late in time behold Him come,
Offspring of the Virgin's womb.
Veiled in flesh the Godhead see;
Hail th' Incarnate Deity,
Pleased as man with men to dwell;
Jesus, our Emmanuel.
Refrain

3. Hail the heavenborn Prince of Peace!
Hail the Sun of Righteousness!
Light and life to all He brings,
Risen with healing in His wings;
Mild He lays His glory by,
Born that man no more may die,
Born to raise the sons of earth,
Born to give them second birth.
Refrain

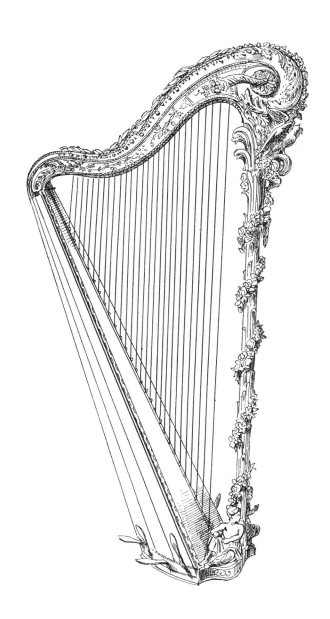

Angels From the Realms of Glory

Words by James Montgomery
(1771–1854)

Henry Smart
(1813–1879)

With spirit

2. Shepherds, in the fields abiding,
 Watching o'er your flocks by night,
 God with man is now residing,
 Yonder shines the infant Light:
  Come and worship, Come and worship,
 Worship Christ, the newborn King!

3. Sages, leave your contemplations,
 Brighter visions beam afar;
 Seek the great Desire of nations;
 Ye have seen His natal star:
  Come and worship, Come and worship,
 Worship Christ, the newborn King!

Bright Angel Hosts Are Heard on High

Traditional Cornish carol

Gaily

1. Bright An - gels hosts are heard on high, All
2. "Say, shep - herds why are this ju - bi - lee? What

sweet - ly sing - ing o'er the plains; While
doth your rap - turous mirth pro - long? Say,

moun - tains ech - o in re - ply The
say what may the tid - ings be, Which

bur - den of their joy - ous strains.
will in - spire that Heav'n - ly song."

3. Come, come to Bethlehem, come and see,
   The Child whose birth the angels sing;
   Come, come, adore on bended knee,
   The Infant Christ, the newborn King!

4. See, there within a manger laid
   Jesus, the Lord of heaven and earth!
   See, saints and angels lend their aid,
   To celebrate the Savior's birth!

Nowell! Nowell!

Traditional German carol

Majestically

1. No - well! No - well! Good news I tell, And

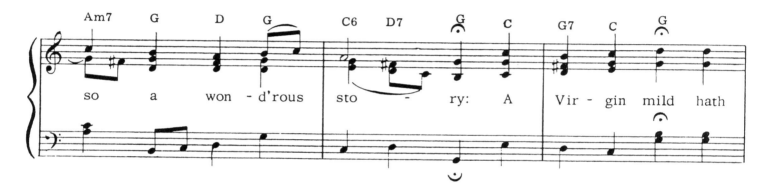

so a won - d'rous sto - ry: A Vir - gin mild hath

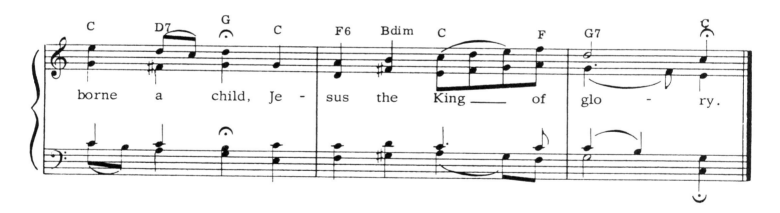

borne a child, Je - sus the King ___ of glo - ry.

2. Ave Marie! O Well is Thee,
   Thou daughter born of Anna,
   Before that Son, that Holy One,
   Archangels sang Hosanna.

3. Then praise be sung and bells be rung,
   To greet this kindly Stranger,
   Th' ancient of days, mankind to raise,
   Abhorreth not the manger.

While Shepherds Watched Their Flocks

Words by Nahum Tate
(1652–1715)

Music by George Frideric Handel
(1685–1759)

2. "Fear not!" said he, for mighty dread
   Had seized their troubled mind,
   "Glad tidings of great joy I bring,
   To you and all mankind,
     To you and all mankind.

3. "To you, in David's town, this day
   Is born of David's line
   The Savior who is Christ the Lord,
   And this shall be the sign,
     And this shall be the sign.

4. "The Heav'nly Babe you there shall find
   To human view displayed,
   All meanly wrapped in swathing band
   And in a manger laid,
     And in a manger laid.

5. "All glory be to God on high,
   And to the earth be peace,
   Good will henceforth from heav'n to men,
   Begin and never cease,
     Begin and never cease."

Rise Up, Shepherd, an' Follow

Traditional African-American spiritual

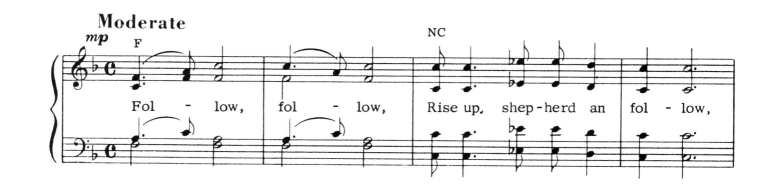

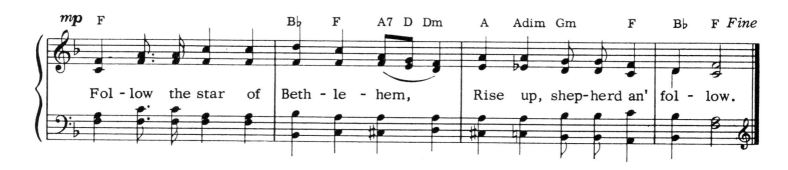

Bring a Torch, Jeannette, Isabella

(Un flambeau, Jeanette, Isabelle)

Traditional French carol

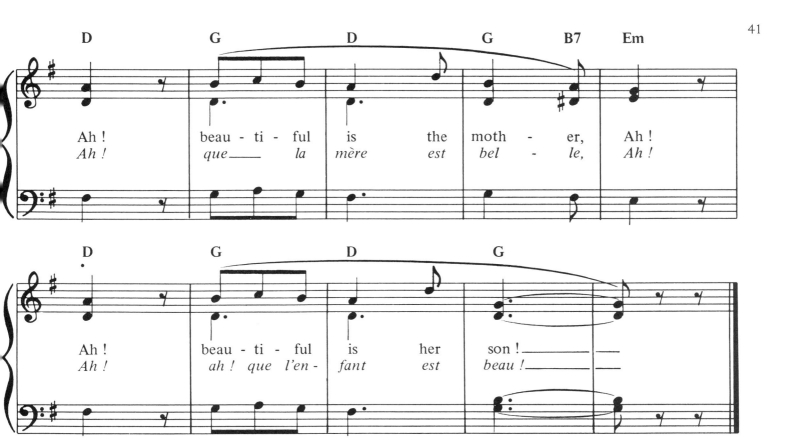

Ah! beau-ti-ful is the moth-er, Ah!
Ah! que___ la mère est bel - le, Ah!

Ah! beau-ti-ful is her son!_____
Ah! ah! que l'en - fant est beau!_____

2. It is wrong when the child is sleeping,
It is wrong to talk so loud;
Silence, all, as you gather around,
Lest your noise should waken Jesus:
Hush! hush! see how fast he slumbers:
Hush! hush! see how fast he sleeps!

3. Softly to the little stable,
Softly for a moment come;
Look and see how charming is Jesus,
How he is white, his cheeks are rosy!
Hush! hush! see how the child is sleeping;
Hush! hush! see how he smiles in his dreams.

While by My Sheep I Watched at Night

Traditional German carol

3. There shall He lie in manger mean,
   Who shall redeem the word from sin.
   Refrain

4. Lord evermore to me be nigh,
   Then shall my heart be filled with joy.
   Refrain

Shepherds! Shake Off Your Drowsy Sleep

Traditional French carol

2. Hark! Even now the bells ring 'round,
   Listen to their merry sound;
   Hark how the birds new songs are making!
   As if winter's chains were breaking.
   Refrain

3. See how the flow'rs all burst anew,
   Thinking snow is summer dew;
   See how the stars afresh are glowing,
   All their brightest beams bestowing.
   Refrain

4. Cometh at length the age of peace,
   Strife and sorrow now shall cease;
   Prophets foretold the wondrous story
   Of this heav'n-born Prince of Glory.
   Refrain

5. Shepherds, then up and quick away,
   Seek the Babe ere break of day;
   He is the hope of every nation,
   All in Him shall find salvation.
   Refrain

Away in a Manger

(first version)

Words Traditional

Music by James R. Murray
(1841–1905)

1. A-way in a man-ger, no crib for a bed, The lit-tle Lord Je-sus laid down his sweet head; The stars in the sky looked down where he lay, The lit-tle Lord Je-sus a-sleep in the hay.

2. The cattle are lowing, the baby awakes,
   But little Lord Jesus, no crying he makes.
   I love thee, Lord Jesus, look down from the sky,
   And stay by my cradle till morning is nigh.

3. Be near me Lord Jesus, I ask thee to stay
   Close by me forever, and love me, I pray.
   Bless all the dear children in thy tender care,
   And fit us for heaven to live with thee there.

Away in a Manger
(second version)

Words Traditional

Music by William J. Kirkpatrick
(1838–1921)

2. The cattle are lowing, the baby awakes,
But little Lord Jesus, no crying he makes.
I love thee, Lord Jesus, look down from the sky,
And stay by my cradle till morning is nigh.

3. Be near me Lord Jesus, I ask thee to stay
Close by me forever, and love me, I pray.
Bless all the dear children in thy tender care,
And fit us for heaven to live with thee there.

What Child Is This?

Words by William Chatterton Dix
(1837–1898)

Traditional English air:
'Greensleeves'

1. What child is this, who, laid to rest, on

Ma - ry's lap is sleep - ing? Whom

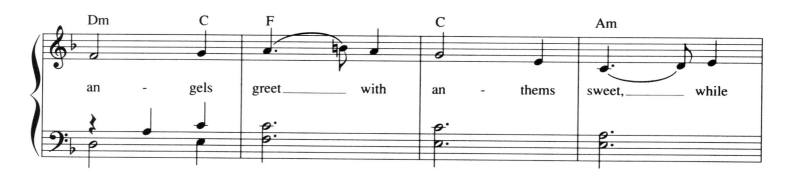

an - gels greet with an - thems sweet, while

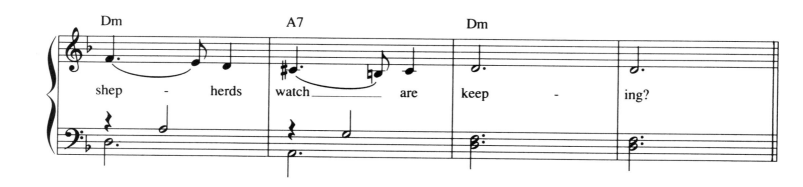

shep - herds watch are keep - ing?

Refrain

2. Why lies He in such mean estate
   Where ox and ass are feeding?
   Good Christian, fear: for sinners here
   The silent Word is pleading.
   Refrain

3. So bring Him incense, gold, and myrrh
   Come peasant, king, to own Him
   The King of Kings salvation brings
   Let loving hearts enthrone Him.
   Refrain

Coventry Carol

Traditional English carol

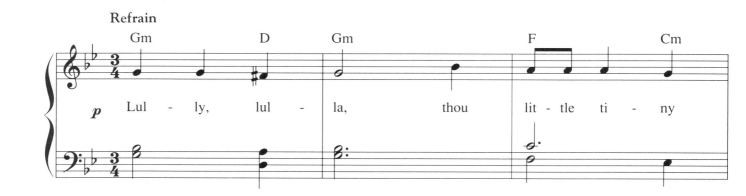

Lul - ly, lul - la, thou lit - tle ti - ny

Child. By, by, lul - ly, lul - lay.

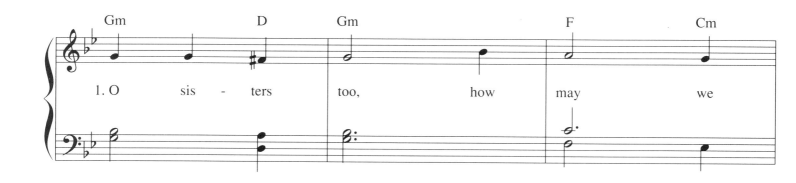

1. O sis - ters too, how may we

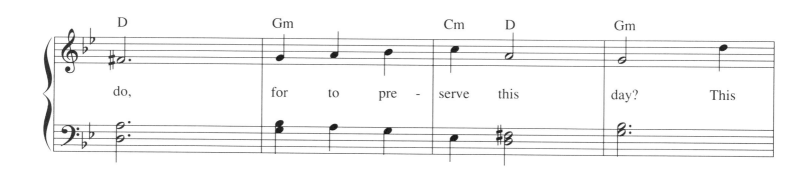

do, for to pre - serve this day? This

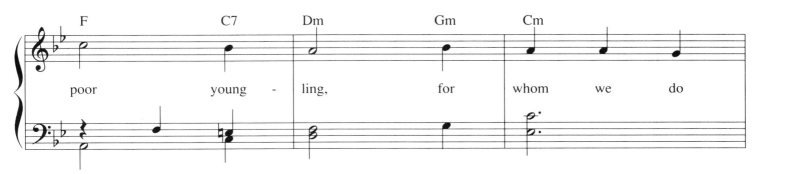

poor young - ling, for whom we do

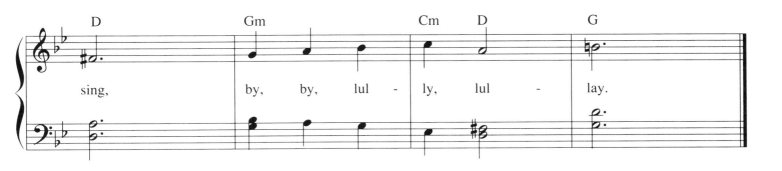

sing, by, by, lul - ly, lul - lay.

2. Herod the king in his raging,
   Chargèd he hath this day
   His men of might, in his own sight,
   All children young to slay.
   Refrain

3. That woe is me, poor Child, for Thee,
   And ever mourn and say,
   For Thy parting nor say nor sing,
   By, by lully, lullay.
   Refrain

The Huron Indian Carol

Traditional Native American carol

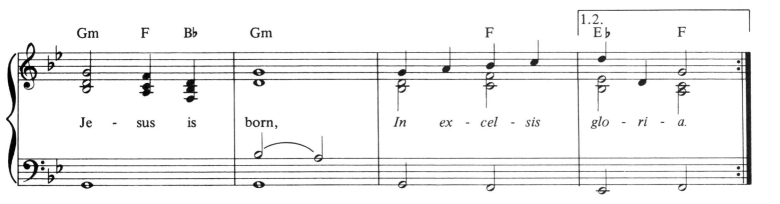

Je - sus is born, In ex - cel - sis glo - ri - a.

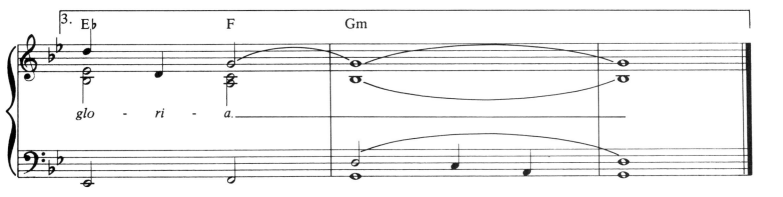

glo - ri - a.

2. Within a lodge of broken bark
   the tender Babe was found,
   A ragged robe of rabbit skin
   enwrapped His beauty round.
   The chiefs from far before Him knelt
   with gifts of fox and beaver pelt.
   Refrain

3. O children of the forest free,
   O sons of Manitou,
   The Holy Child of earth and heav'n
   is born today for you,
   Come kneel before the radiant Boy
   who brings you beauty, peace and joy.
   Refrain

Infant Holy, Infant Lowly

Traditional Polish carol

2. Flocks were sleeping, shepherds keeping
   Vigil till the morning new,
   Saw the glory, heard the story,
   Tidings of a gospel true.
   Thus rejoicing, free from sorrow,
   Praises voicing, greet the morrow,
   Christ the babe was born for you,
   Christ the babe was born for you.

Slumber Song of the Infant Jesus

Words by H.R. Wilson

Music by François A. Gevaert
(1828–1908)

2. Mid lilies white and roses red,
   Sleep, sleep, in Thy lowly bed,
   Refrain

3. While gentle shepherds kneel in prayer,
   Sleep, sleep, my Child so fair.
   Refrain

The Friendly Beasts

Traditional English carol

3. "I," said the cow, all white and red,
   "I have Him my manger for his bed.
   I gave Him hay to pillow his head."
   "I," said the cow, all white and red.

4. "I," said the sheep, with curly horn,
   "I gave Him my wool for his blanket warm;
   He wore my coat on Christmas morn."
   "I," said the sheep, with curly horn.

5. "I," said the dove, from rafters high,
   "Cooed Him to sleep that He should not cry;
   We cooed Him to sleep, my mate and I."
   "I," said the dove, from rafters high.

6. Thus every beast by some good spell
   In the stable dark was glad to tell
   Of the gift he gave Emmanuel,
   The gift he gave Emmanuel.

Lullaby Carol

Traditional Polish carol

Beside Thy Manger, Here I Stand

Words by Martin Luther
(1483–1546)

Traditional German tune

Whence Comes This Rush of Wings?

Traditional French carol

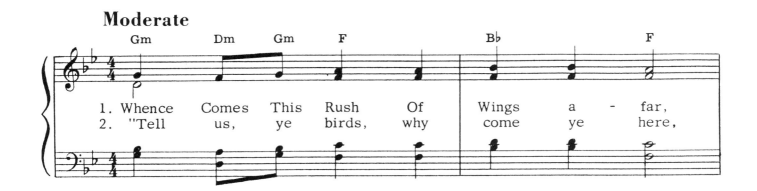

1. Whence Comes This Rush Of Wings a - far,
2. "Tell us, ye birds, why come ye here,

Fol - low - ing straight the No - el star? Birds from the woods in
In - to this sta - ble poor and drear?" "Hast -'ning we seek the

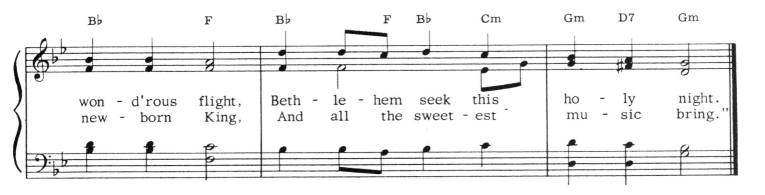

won - d'rous flight, Beth - le - hem seek this ho - ly night.
new - born King, And all the sweet - est mu - sic bring."

3. Hark, how the greenfinch bears his part!
   Philomel, too, with tender heart,
   Chants from her leafy dark retreat,
   Re, mi, fa, sol, in accents sweet.

4. Angels and shepherds, birds of the sky,
   Come where the Son of God doth lie;
   Christ on earth with man doth dwell,
   Join in the shout, "Noel, Noel!"

Rocking

Traditional Czech carol

Cradle Hymn

Words by Isaac Watts
(1674–1748)

Music by Jean-Jacques Rousseau
(1712–1778)

1. Hush, my babe, lie still and slumber, Holy angels guard thy bed.
2. Soft and easy is thy cradle, Coarse and hard thy Saviour lay:
3. Hush, my child, I did not chide thee, Though my song may seem so hard:

Heav'n-ly bless-ings with-out num-ber, Gent-ly fall-ing on thy head.
When His birth-place was a sta-ble And his soft-est bed was hay.
'Tis thy moth-er sits be-side thee, And her arms shall be thy guard,

How much bet-ter thou'rt at-tend-ed, Than the Son of God could be;
Oh, to tell the won-drous sto-ry, How his foes a-bused their King;
May'st thou learn to know and fear Him, Love and serve Him all thy days;

When from heav-en He de-scend-ed, And be-came a child like thee.
How they killed the Lord of glo-ry, Makes me an-gry while I sing.
Then to dwell for-ev-er near Him, Tell his love and sing His praise.

Once in Royal David's City

Mrs. Cecil Frances Alexander
(1823–1895)

Music by Henry John Gauntlett
(1805–1876)

mf 1. Once in Roy - al Dav - id's ci - ty stood a

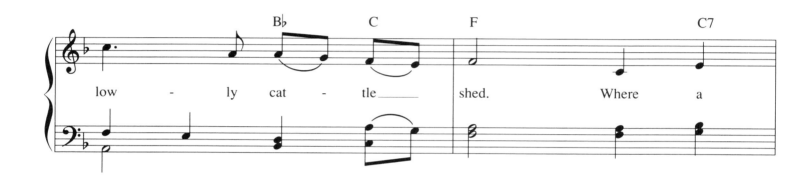

low - ly cat - tle shed. Where a

moth - er laid her ba - by, in a

man - ger for His bed. Ma - ry

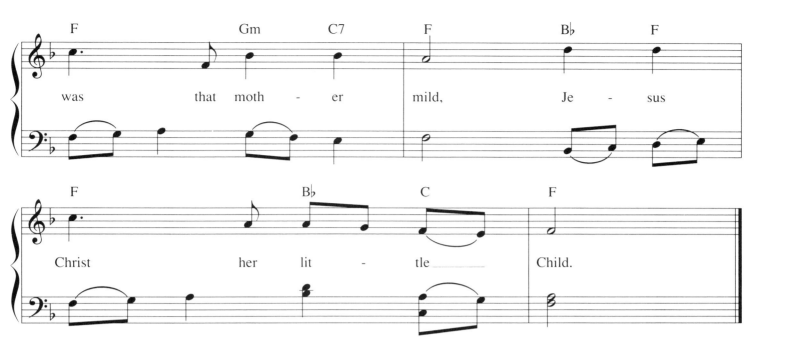

was that moth - er mild, Je - sus

Christ her lit - tle _____ Child.

2. He came down to earth from heaven
   Who is God and Lord of all,
   And His shelter was a stable,
   And His cradle was a stall.
   With the poor and mean and lowly
   Lived on earth our Savior holy.

3. And through all His wondrous childhood
   He would honor and obey,
   Love and watch the lowly maiden,
   In whose gentle arms He lay.
   Christian children all must be,
   Mild, obedient, good as He.

4. For He is our childhood's pattern,
   Day by day like us He grew,
   He was little, weak and helpless,
   Tears and smiles like us He knew,
   And He feeleth for our sadness,
   And He shareth in our gladness.

5. And our eyes at last shall see Him,
   Through His own redeeming love,
   For that Child so dear and gentle
   Is our Lord in heaven above,
   And He leads his children on
   To the place where He is gone.

6. Not in that poor lowly stable,
   With the oxen standing by,
   We shall see Him, but in heaven
   Set at God's right hand on high,
   Where, like stars, His children crowned
   All in white shall wait around.

See Amid the Winter's Snow

Words by Edward Caswell
(1814–1878)

Music by John Goss
(1800–1880)

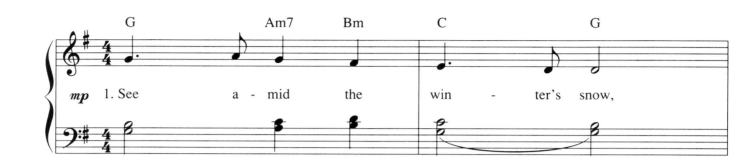

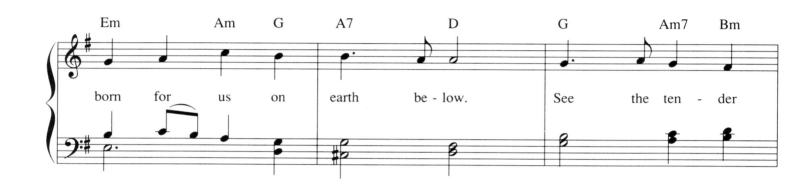

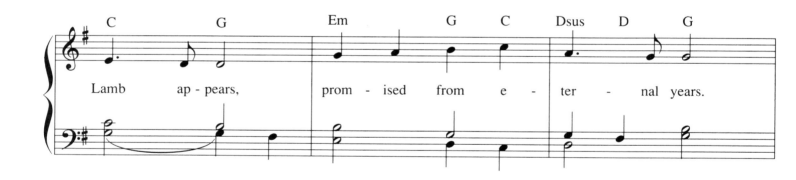

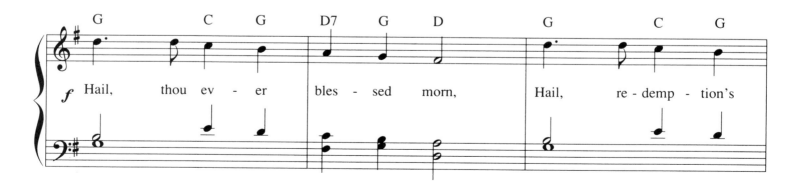

hap - py dawn. Sing through all Je - ru - sa - lem,

Christ is born in Beth - le - hem.

2. Lo, within a manger lies
   He who built the starry skies;
   He, who throned in height sublime,
   Sits amid the Cherubim.
       Refrain

3. Say, ye holy shepherds, say
   What your joyful news today;
   Wherefore have ye left your sheep
   On the lonely mountain steep?
       Refrain

4. "As we watched at dead of night,
   Lo, we saw a wondrous light;
   Angels singing peace on earth
   Told us of the Savior's birth."
       Refrain

5. Sacred Infant, all divine,
   What a tender love was Thine;
   Thus to come from highest bliss
   Down to such a world as this.
       Refrain

6. Teach, O teach us, Holy Child,
   By thy face so meek and mild,
   Teach us to resemble Thee
   In Thy sweet humility.
       Refrain

The Seven Joys of Mary

Traditional English carol

2. The next good joy that Mary had,
   It was the joy of two,
   To see her own Son, Jesus Christ,
   Making the lame to go.
       Refrain:
       Making the lame to go, *etc.*

3. The next good joy that Mary had,
   It was the joy of three,
   To see her own Son, Jesus Christ,
   Making the blind to see.
       Refrain:
       Making the blind to see, *etc.*

4. The next good joy that Mary had,
   It was the joy of four,
   To see her own Son, Jesus Christ,
   Reading the Bible o'er.
       Refrain:
       Reading the Bible o'er, *etc.*

5. The next good joy that Mary had,
   It was the joy of five,
   To see her own Son, Jesus Christ,
   Raising the dead to life.
       Refrain:
       Raising the dead to life, *etc.*

6. The next good joy that Mary had,
   It was the joy of six,
   To see her own Son, Jesus Christ,
   Upon the Crucifix.
       Refrain:
       Upon the Crucifix, *etc.*

7. The next good joy that Mary had,
   It was the joy of seven,
   To see her own Son, Jesus Christ,
   Ascending into Heav'n.
       Refrain:
       Ascending into Heav'n, *etc.*

Joseph Dearest, Joseph Mine

Traditional German carol

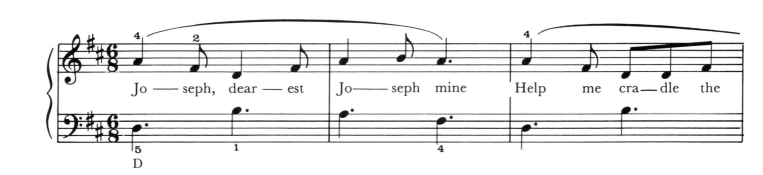

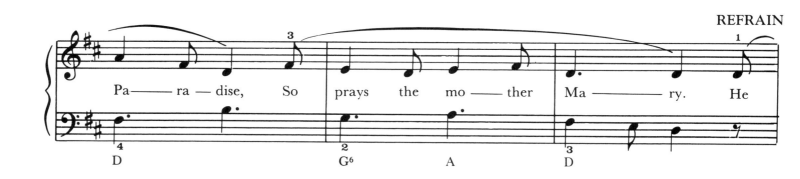

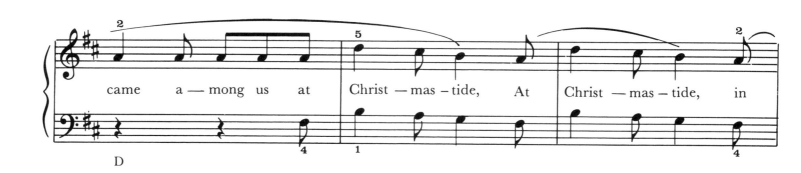

Beth — le — hem; Men shall bring Him from far and wide Love's

Esus E A D

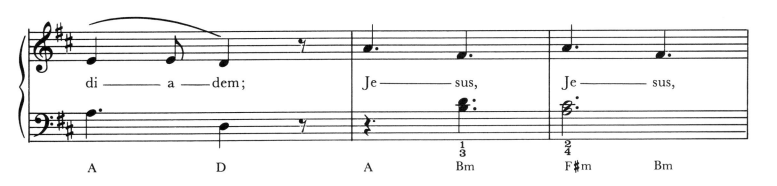

di — a — dem; Je — sus, Je — sus,

A D A Bm F#m Bm

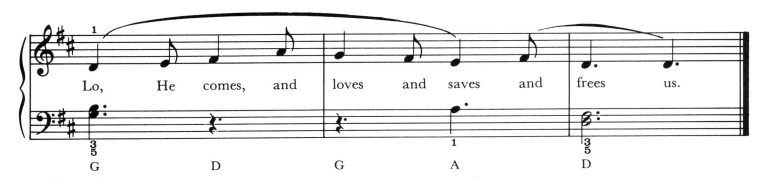

Lo, He comes, and loves and saves and frees us.

G D G A D

2. Gladly, dear one, lady mine,
Help I cradle this child of thine;
God's own light on us both shall shine
In Paradise,
As prays the mother Mary.
Refrain

3. Peace to all that have goodwill,
God who heaven and earth doth fill,
Comes to turn us away from ill,
And lies so still
Within the crib of Mary.
Refrain

4. All shall come and bow the knee,
Wise and happy their souls shall be,
Loving such a divinity,
As all may see
In Jesus, son of Mary.
Refrain

5. Now is born Emmanuel,
Prophesied once by Ezekiel,
Promised Mary by Gabriel—
Ah, who can tell
Thy praises, son of Mary.
Refrain

6. Thou my lazy heart has stirred,
Thou, the Father's eternal word,
Greater than aught that ear hath heard,
Thou tiny bird
Of love, thou son of Mary.
Refrain

Mary Had a Baby

Traditional African-American spiritual

3. Laid Him in a manger, oh, Lord,
   Laid Him in a manger, oh, Lord,
   Laid Him in a manger, laid Him in a manger,
   Laid Him in a manger, oh, Lord,

4. What did she name Him? oh, Lord,
   What did she name Him? oh, Lord,
   What did she name Him? What did she name Him?
   What did she name Him? oh, Lord,

5. Named Him King Jesus, oh, Lord,
   Named Him King Jesus, oh, Lord,
   Named Him King Jesus, named Him King Jesus,
   Named Him King Jesus, oh, Lord.

6. Who heard the singing? oh, Lord,
   Who heard the singing? oh, Lord,
   Who heard the singing? Who heard the singing?
   Who heard the singing? oh, Lord.

7. Shepherds heard the singing, oh, Lord,
   Shepherds heard the singing, oh, Lord,
   Shepherds heard the singing, shepherds heard the singing,
   Shepherds heard the singing, oh, Lord.

8. Star kept a-shining, oh, Lord,
   Star kept a-shining, oh, Lord,
   Star kept a-shining, star kept a-shining,
   Star kept a-shining, oh, Lord.

Mary Had a Boychild

Traditional West Indian carol

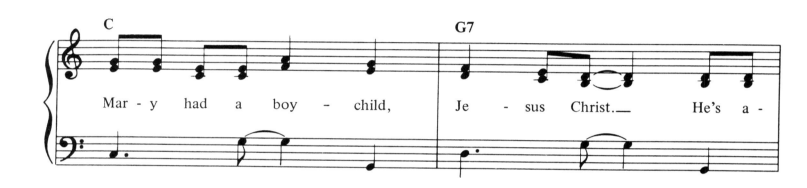

Verse

Long time a - go in Beth - le - hem, ___ so the
Ho - ly Bi - ble say, Mar - y's boy - child
Je - sus Christ ___ was born on Christ - mas Day!

A Virgin Most Pure

Traditional English carol

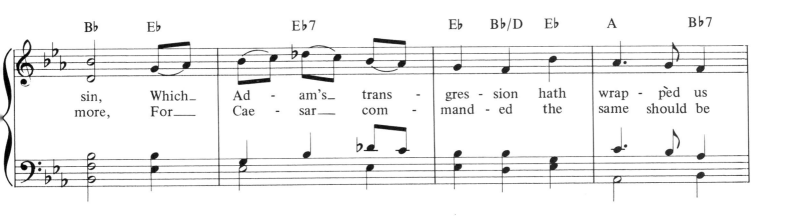

sin, Which Ad-am's trans - gres - sion hath wrap - pèd us
more, For Cae - sar com - mand - ed the same should be

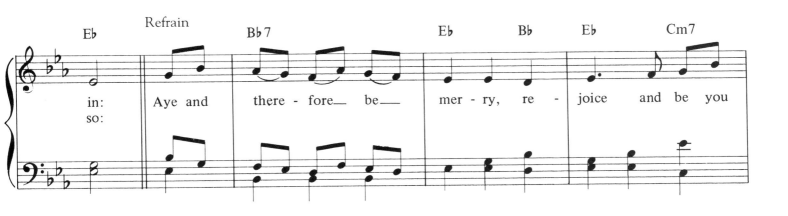

Refrain

in: Aye and there - fore be mer - ry, re - joice and be you
so:

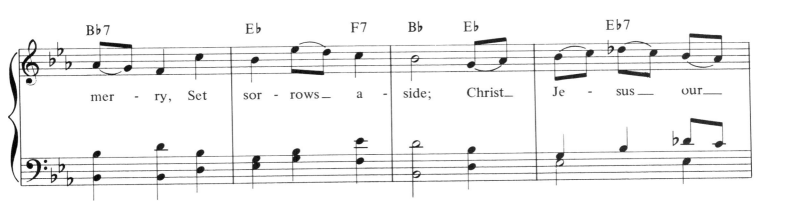

mer - ry, Set sor - rows a - side; Christ Je - sus our

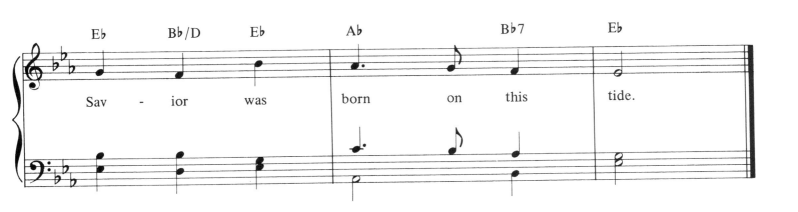

Sav - ior was born on this tide.

3. But when they had entered the city so fair,
   A number of people so mighty was there
   That Joseph and Mary, whose substance was small,
   Could find in the inn there no lodging at all.
   Refrain

4. Then were they constrained in a stable to lie,
   Where the horses and asses they used for to tie;
   Their lodging so simple they took it no scorn:
   But against the next morning our Savior was born:
   Refrain

5. The King of all kings to this world being brought,
   Small store of fine linen to wrap Him was sought;
   And when she had swaddled her young son so sweet,
   Within an ox-manger she laid Him to sleep:
   Refrain

6. Then God sent an angel from heaven so high
   To certain poor shepherds in fields where they lie,
   And bade them no longer in sorrow to stay,
   Because that our Savior was born on this day;
   Refrain

7. Then presently after the shepherds did spy
   A number of angels that stood in the sky;
   They joyfully talkèd, and sweetly did sing
   To God be all glory, our heavenly King:
   Refrain

As With Gladness Men of Old

Words by William Chatterton Dix
(1837–1898)

Music by Konrad Kocher
(1786–1872)

We Three Kings of Orient Are

Words and music by John Henry Hopkins
(1820–1891)

2. Born a King on Bethlehem's plain,
   Gold I bring to crown Him again,
   King forever, ceasing never
   Over us all to reign.
   Refrain

3. Frankincense to offer have I,
   Incense owns a deity nigh:
   Prayer and praising, all men raising,
   Worship Him, God on high.
   Refrain

4. Myrrh is mine; its bitter perfume
   Breathes a life of gathering gloom;
   Sorrowing, sighing, bleeding, dying,
   Sealed in a stone cold tomb.
   Refrain

5. Glorious now behold Him arise,
   King and God, and sacrifice.
   Alleluia, Alleluia!
   Sounds through the earth and skies.
   Refrain

Behold That Star

Traditional African-American spiritual

Eastern Monarchs, Sages Three

Traditional English carol

Moderate

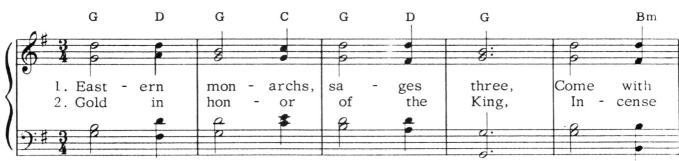

1. East - ern mon - archs, sa - ges three, Come with
2. Gold in hon - or of the King, In - cense

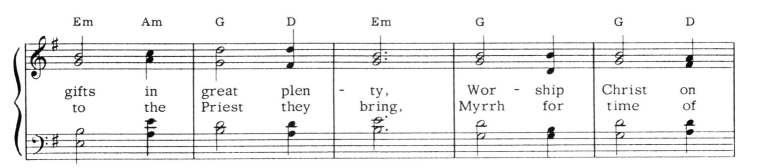

gifts in great plen - ty, Wor - ship Christ on
to the Priest they bring, Myrrh for time of

bend - ed knee, *Cum Vir - gi - ne Ma - ri - a.*
bur - y - ing,

3. On that dreadful day, the last,
   He forgave our sinful past.
   To His mercy cling we fast,
   Cum Virgine Maria

4. On His might, it hath no end,
   All created things depend,
   To His will, the world must bend,
   Cum Virgine Maria

5. His the praise and glory be,
   Laud and honours, victory,
   Pow'r supreme! and so sing we,
   Cum Virgine Maria

6. On the feast-day of His birth
   Set on thrones above the earth.
   Angels chant in holy mirth,
   Cum Virgine Maria

7. Thus to bless the One in Three,
   Let this present company
   Raise the voice of melody,
   Cum Virgine Maria

Brightest and Best

Words Traditional

Music by Felix Mendelssohn
(1809–1847)

3. Say, shall we yield Him, in costly devotion,
   Odors of Edom, and off'rings divine,
   Gems of the mountain, and pearls of the ocean,
   Myrrh from the forest and gold from the mine?

4. Vainly we offer each ample oblation,
   Vainly with gifts would His favor secure;
   Richer, by far, is the heart's adoration
   Dearer to God are the prayers of the poor.

Star of the East

Words by George Cooper

Music by Amanda Kennedy

Star of the East, Oh Beth-le-hem's star, Guid-ing us on to Heav-en a-far!
Star of the East, un-dim'd by each cloud, What tho' the storms of grief gath-er loud?

Sor-row and grief are lull'd by thy light, Thou hope of each mor-tal, in death's lone-ly night!
Faith-ful and pure thy rays beam to save, Still bright o'er the cra-dle, and bright o'er the grave!

O Come All Ye Faithful

Traditional English carol

Refrain

O come, let us a-dore Him, O come let us a-dore Him, O come let us a-dore Him, — Christ the — Lord.

2. Sing, choirs of angels, sing in exultation,
   O sing all ye citizens of heaven above!
   Glory to God, all Glory in the highest.
   Refrain

3. Yea, Lord, we greet Thee, born this happy morning,
   Jesus, to Thee be all glory giv'n;
   Word of the Father, now in flesh appearing.
   Refrain

How Far Is It to Bethlehem?

Traditional American carol

p 1. How___ far is it to Beth - le - hem?

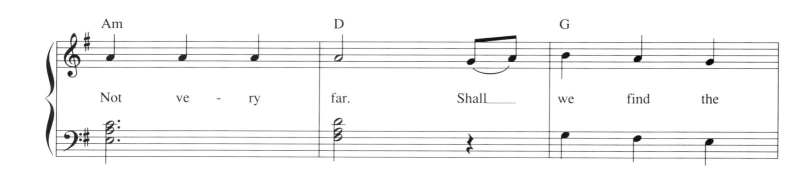

Not ve - ry far. Shall___ we find the

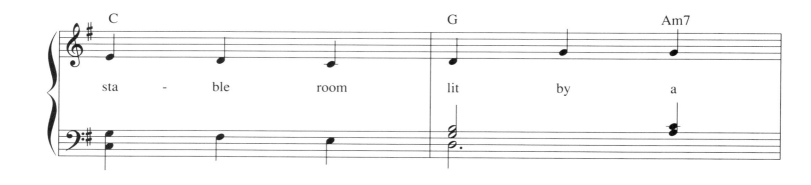

sta - ble room lit by a

star? Can we see the lit - tle Child,

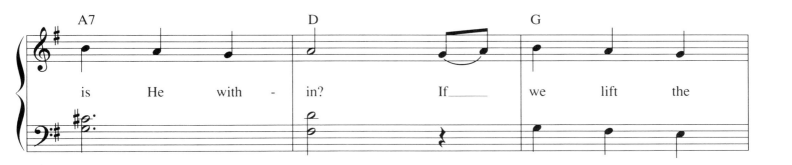

is He with - in? If_____ we lift the

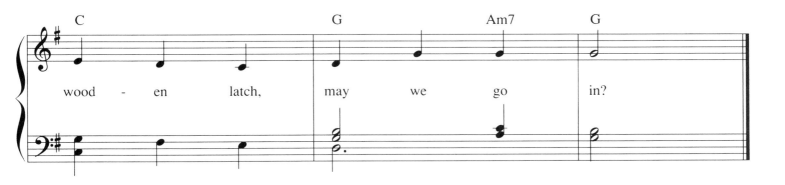

wood - en latch, may we go in?

2. May we stroke the creatures there, ox, ass or sheep?
   May we peep like them and see Jesus asleep?
   If we touch His tiny hand, will He awake?
   Will He know we've come so far just for His sake?

3. Great kings have precious gifts, and we have naught.
   Little smiles and little tears are all we have brought.
   For all weary children, Mary must weep,
   Here on His bed of straw, sleep, children, sleep.

O Come, O Come Emmanuel

Traditional French carol

Refrain

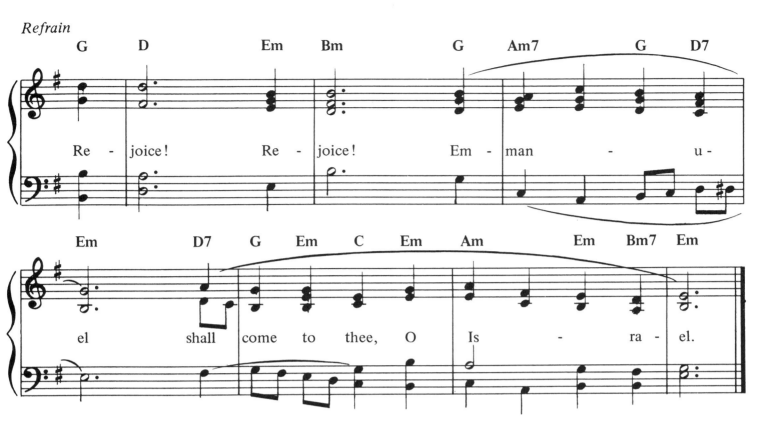

Re - joice! Re - joice! Em - man - u - el shall come to thee, O Is - ra - el.

2. O come, Thou Wisdom from on high,
   And order all things, far and nigh;
   To us the path of knowledge show,
   And cause us in her ways to go.
   Refrain

3. O come, Desire of nations, bind
   All peoples in one heart and mind;
   Bid envy, strife, and quarrels cease;
   Fill the whole world with heaven's peace.
   Refrain

4. O come, Thou Day-spring, come and cheer
   Our spirits by Thine advent here;
   Disperse the gloomy clouds of night,
   And death's dark shadows put to flight.
   Refrain

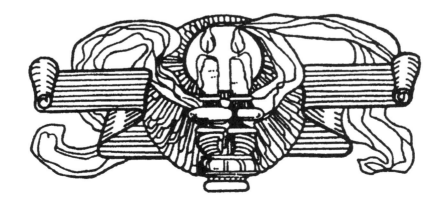

Christians Awake

Words by John Byrom
(1692–1763)

Music by John Wainwright
(1723–1768)

3. To Bethlehem straight the enlightened shepherds ran
   To see the wonder God had wrought for man,
   And found, with Joseph and the Blessed Maid,
   Her Son, the Savior, in a manger laid:
   Then to their flocks, still praising God, return,
   And their glad hearts with holy rapture burn.

4. O may we keep and ponder in our mind
   God's wondrous love in saving lost mankind;
   Trace we the Babe, who hath retrieved our loss,
   From His poor manger to His bitter cross;
   Tread in His steps, assisted by His Grace,
   Till man's first heavenly state again takes place.

5. Then may we hope, the angelic hosts among,
   To sing, redeemed, a glad triumphal song;
   He that was born upon this joyful day
   Around us all His glory shall display;
   Saved by His love, incessant we shall sing
   Eternal praise to heaven's almighty King.

O Come Little Children

Words and music by Johann A.P. Schulz
(1747–1800)

Moderate

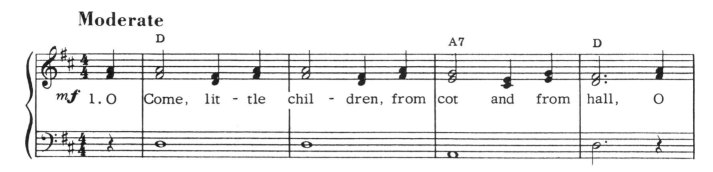

mf 1. O Come, lit - tle chil - dren, from cot and from hall, O

come to the man - ger in Beth - le - hem's stall. There

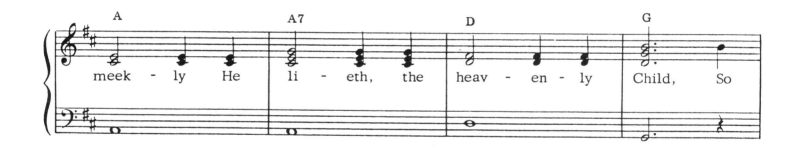

meek - ly He li - eth, the heav - en - ly Child, So

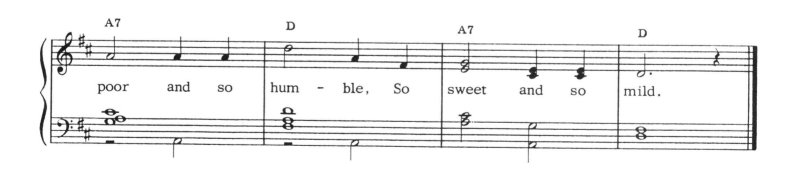

poor and so hum - ble, So sweet and so mild.

2. The hay is His pillow, the manger His bed,
   The beasts stand in wonder to gaze on His head,
   Yet there where He lieth, so weak and so poor,
   Come shepherds and wise men to kneel at His door.

3. Now "Glory to God!" sing the angels on high,
   And "Peace upon earth!" heav'nly voices reply.
   Then come, little children, and join in the lay
   That gladdened the world on that first Christmas Day.

Children, Go Where I Send Thee

Traditional African-American spiritual

Child - ren, go where I send thee. How shall I tell thee?

I'm gon-na send thee one by one. One for the lit-tle bit-ty ba - by, was born, born,

born in Beth - le - hem. I'm gon-na send thee two by two. Two for Paul and Pe - ter.

One for the lit - tle bit - ty ba - by, was born, born, born in Beth - le - hem.

3. I'm gonna send thee three by three.
   Three for the Hebrew children.
   Two for Paul and Silas, *etc.*

4. I'm gonna send thee four by four.
   Four for the four that stood at the door.
   Three for the Hebrew children, *etc.*

5. I'm gonna send thee five by five.
   Five for the Gospel preachers.
   Four for the four that stood at the door, *etc.*

6. I'm gonna send thee six by six.
   Six for the six that never got fixed,
   Five for the Gospel preachers, *etc.*

7. I'm gonna send thee seven by seven.
   Seven for the seven that never got to heaven.
   Six for the six that never got fixed, *etc.*

8. I'm gonna send thee eight by eight.
   Eight for the eight that stood at the gate.
   Seven for the seven that never got to heaven, *etc.*

9. I'm gonna send thee nine by nine.
   Nine for the nine all dressed so fine.
   Eight for the eight that stood at the gate, *etc.*

10. I'm gonna send thee ten by ten.
    Ten for the ten commandments.
    Nine for the nine all dressed so fine, *etc.*

Adoramus Te, Christe

Words Traditional

Music by Giovanni Pierluigi da Palestrina
(c. 1525–1594)

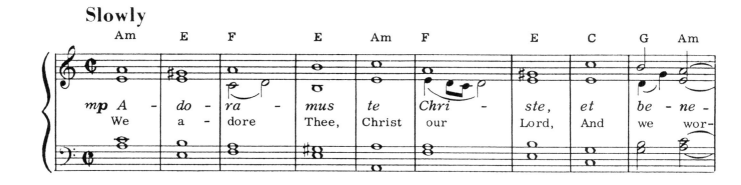

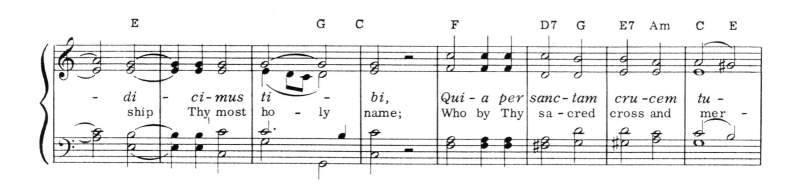

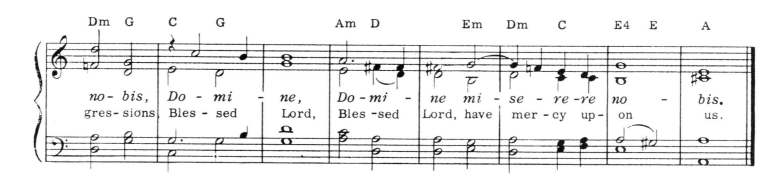

Unto Us a Boy Is Born

Traditional German carol

3. Herod then with fear was filled:
   "A prince," he said, "in Jewry!"
   All the little boys he killed
   At Bethlehem in his fury.

4. Now may Mary's son, who came
   So long ago to love us,
   Lead us all with hearts aflame
   Unto the joys above us.

5. Omega and Alpha he!
   Let the organ thunder,
   While the choir with peals of glee
   Doth rend the air asunder.

Joy to the World

Words by Isaac Watts
(1674–1748)

Traditional English
tune: 'Antioch'

Majestically

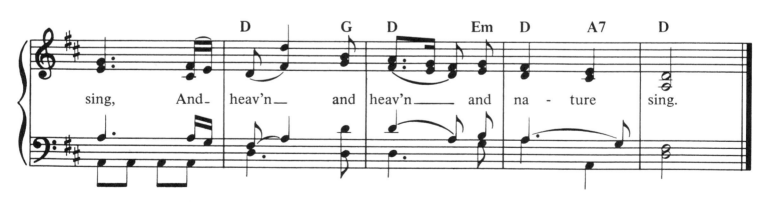

2. Joy to the world! The Savior reigns;
   Let men their songs employ;
   While fields and floods, rocks, hills and plains
   Repeat the sounding joy,
   Repeat the sounding joy,
   Repeat, repeat the sounding joy.

3. He rules the world with truth and grace,
   And makes the nations prove
   The glories of His righteousness,
   And wonders of His love,
   And wonders of His love,
   And wonders, wonders of His love.

Fum, Fum, Fum

Traditional Spanish carol

Moderately

1. On this joy-ful Christ-mas Day, sing fum, fum, fum.

On this joy-ful Christ-mas Day, sing fum, fum, fum. For a

bles-sed Babe was born, Up-on this day at break of morn. In a

man-ger poor and low-ly, Lay the Son of God most ho-ly, fum, fum, fum!

2. Thanks to God for holidays, sing fum, fum, fum.
   Thanks to God for holidays, sing fum, fum, fum.
   Now we all our voices raise, And sing a song of grateful praise,
   Celebrate in song and story, All the wonders of His glory,
   Fum, fum, fum.

God Rest You Merry, Gentlemen

Traditional English carol

1. God rest you mer - ry, gen - tle - men, let noth - ing you dis-
may, Re - mem - ber Christ our Sav - ior was
born on Christ - mas Day, To save us all from
Sa - tan's pow'r when we were gone a - stray;

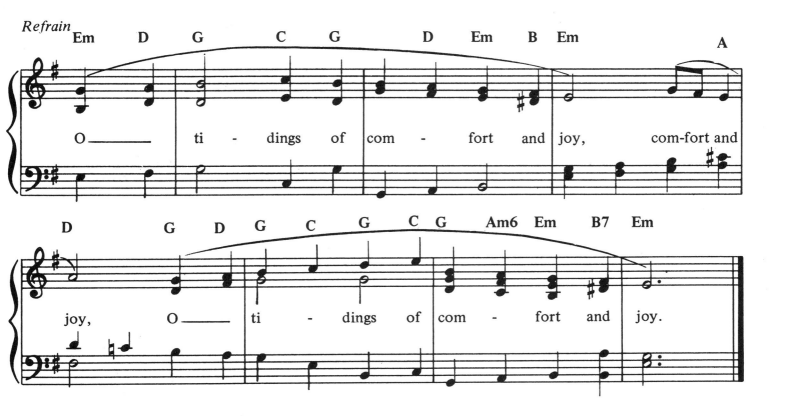

Refrain

O _____ ti - dings of com - fort and joy, com-fort and joy, O _____ ti - dings of com - fort and joy.

2. In Bethlehem in Jewry
   This blessèd babe was born
   And laid within a manger
   Upon this blessèd morn;
   The which his mother Mary
   Nothing did take in scorn:
   Refrain

3. From God our heavenly Father
   A blessèd angel came.
   And unto certain shepherds
   Brought tidings of the same,
   How that in Bethlehem was born
   The Son of God by name:
   Refrain

4. "Fear not," then said the angel,
   "Let nothing you affright,
   This day is born a Savior,
   Of virtue, power, and might;
   So frequently to vanquish all
   The friends of Satan quite:"
   Refrain

5. The shepherds at those tidings
   Rejoicèd much in mind,
   And left their flocks a-feeding,
   In tempest, storm, and wind,
   And went to Bethlehem straightway
   This blessèd babe to find:
   Refrain

6. But when to Bethlehem they came,
   Whereat this infant lay
   They found him in a manger,
   Where oxen feed on hay;
   His mother Mary kneeling,
   Unto the Lord did pray:
   Refrain

7. Now to the Lord sing praises,
   All you within this place,
   And with true love and brotherhood
   Each other now embrace;
   This holy tide of Christmas
   All others doth deface:
   Refrain

I Saw Three Ships

Traditional English carol

3. Our Savior Christ and his lady,
   On Christmas Day, on Christmas Day,
   Our Savior Christ and his lady,
   On Christmas Day in the morning.

4. Pray, whither sailed those ships all three? *etc.*

5. O, they sailed into Bethlehem,

6. And all the bells on earth shall ring,

7. And all the angels in heav'n shall sing,

8. And all the souls on earth shall sing,

9. Then let us all rejoice amain!

Good Christian Men, Rejoice

Traditional German carol

2. Good Christian men, rejoice,
   With heart and soul and voice;
   Now ye hear of endless bliss; Joy! Joy!
   Jesus Christ was born for this!
   He hath op'n'd the heavenly door,
   And man is blessèd evermore.
   Christ was born for this,
   Christ was born for this!

3. Good Christian men, rejoice,
   With heart and soul and voice;
   Now ye need not fear the grave; Peace! Peace!
   Jesus Christ was born to save!
   Calls you one and calls you all,
   To gain his everlasting hall.
   Christ was born to save,
   Christ was born to save!

The Happy Christmas Comes Once More

Traditional Scandinavian carol

Gayly

p 1. The Hap - py Christ - mas Comes Once More, The heav'n - ly

Guest is — at — the door. The bles - sed words the

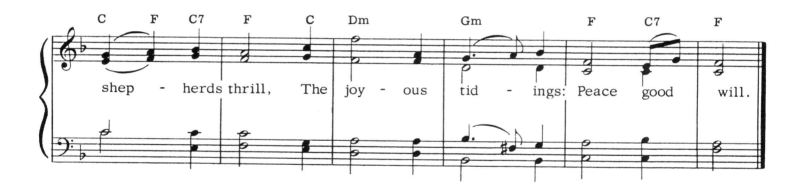

shep - herds thrill, The joy - ous tid - ings: Peace good will.

2. To David's city let us fly,
   Where angels sing beneath the sky;
   Through plain and village pressing near,
   And news from God with shepherds near.

3. O wake our hearts, in gladness sing,
   And keep our Christmas with our King,
   'Til living song, from loving souls,
   Like sound of mighty water rolls.

Rejoice and Be Merry

Traditional English carol

2. A heavenly vision appeared in the sky;
   Vast numbers of angels the shepherds did spy,
   Proclaiming the birthday of Jesus our King,
   Who brought us salvation—His praises we'll sing!

3. Likewise a bright star in the sky did appear,
   Which led the wise men from the East to draw near;
   They found the Messiah, sweet Jesus our King,
   Who brought us salvation—His praises we'll sing!

4. And when they were come, they their treasures unfold,
   And unto Him offered myrrh, incense, and gold.
   So blessèd forever be Jesus our King,
   Who brought us salvation—His praises we'll sing!

A Child This Day Is Born

Traditional English carol

2. These tidings shepherds heard,
Whilst watching o'er their fold,
Were by an angel unto them
That night revealed and told.
Refrain

3. To whom the angel spoke
Saying, "Be not afraid;
Be glad, poor blessèd shepherds.
Why are you so dismayed?"
Refrain

4. "For lo! I bring you tidings
Of gladness and of mirth,
Which cometh to all people by
This holy infant's birth."
Refrain

5. All glory be to God
And His celestial King;
All glory be in Paradise,
This heav'nly host did sing.
Refrain

As Each Happy Christmas

Traditional German carol

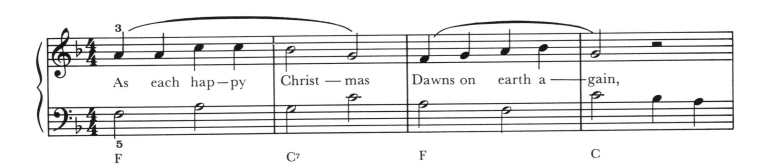

As each hap—py Christ—mas Dawns on earth a——gain,

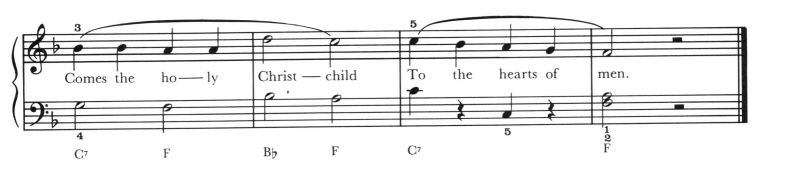

Comes the ho——ly Christ——child To the hearts of men.

2. Enters with His blessing
Into ev'ry home,
Guides and guards our footsteps,
As we go and come.

3. All unknown, beside me
He will ever stand,
And will safely lead me,
With His own right hand.

Go Tell It on the Mountain

Traditional African-American spiritual

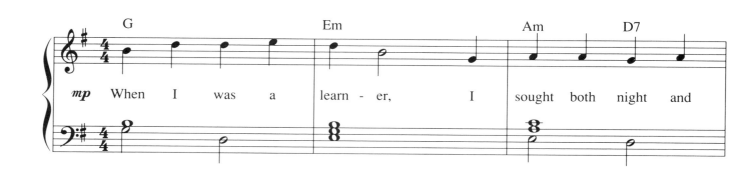

mp When I was a learn - er, I sought both night and

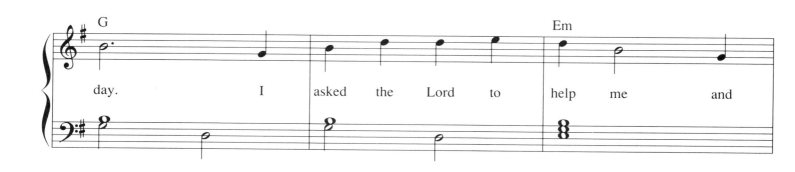

day. I asked the Lord to help me and

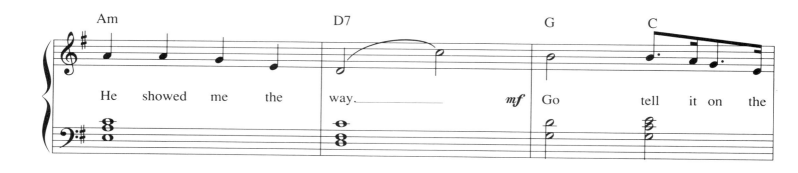

He showed me the way. *mf* Go tell it on the

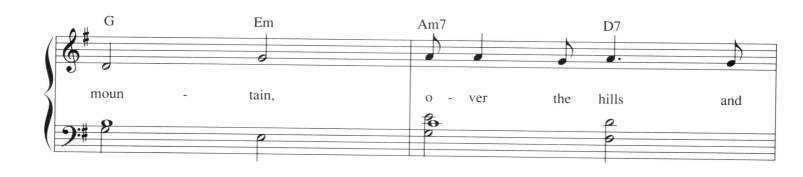

moun - tain, o - ver the hills and

ev - ery - where._____ Go tell it on the moun - tain that

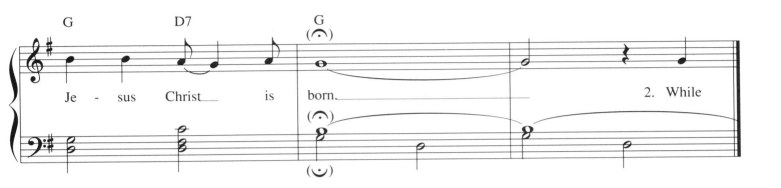

Je - sus Christ___ is born._____ 2. While

2. While shepherds kept their watching,
   O'er wand'ring flock by night;
   Behold! from out of heaven,
   There shown a holy light.
     Refrain

3. And lo, when they had seen it,
   They all bowed down and prayed;
   Then they travelled on together,
   To where the Babe was laid.
     Refrain

4. He made me a watchman,
   Upon the city wall,
   And if I am a Christian
   I am the least of all.
     Refrain

Oh Thou Joyful Day

Traditional German carol

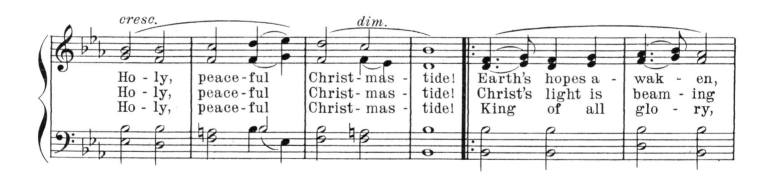

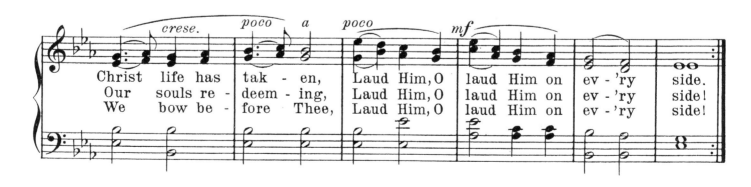

Dona Nobis Pacem

Traditional German carol

Jingle Bells

Words and music by James S. Pierpont
(1822–1893)

REFRAIN

Jin - gle bells! Jin - gle bells! Jin - gle all the

way! Oh, what fun it is to ride In a

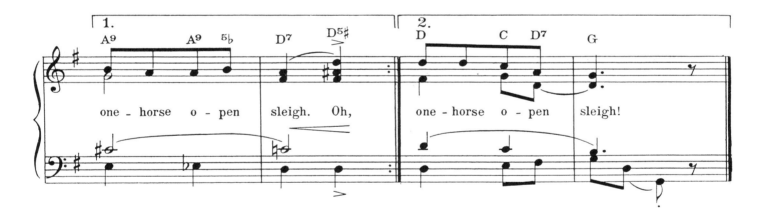

1. one - horse o - pen sleigh. Oh,

2. one - horse o - pen sleigh!

2. A day or two ago
   I thought I'd take a ride,
   Soon Miss Fanny Bright
   Was seated at my side.
   The horse was lean and lank,
   Misfortune seemed his lot,
   He got into a drifted bank,
   And we, we got upsot!
   Refrain

3. Now the ground is white,
   Go it while you're young!
   Take the girls tonight,
   And sing this sleighing song.
   Just get a bobtailed bay,
   Two-forty for his speed,
   Then hitch him to an open sleigh
   And crack! you'll take the lead.
   Refrain

Ding Dong, Merrily on High

Words Traditional

Music by Thoinot Arbeau
(1520–1595)

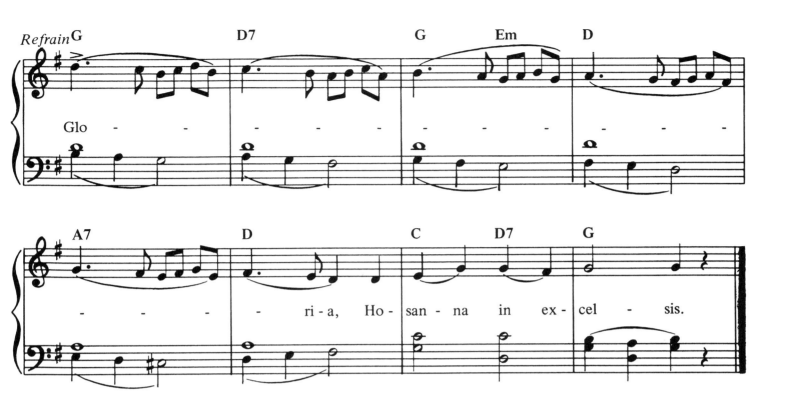

Refrain G   D7   G   Em   D

Glo - - - - - - -

A7   D   C   D7   G

- - - - ri - a, Ho - san - na in ex - cel - sis.

3. Praise Him! people far and near,
   And join the angels' singing.
   Ding dong, everywhere we hear
   The Christmas bells a-ringing
   Refrain

4. Hear them ring this happy morn!
   Our God a gift has given;
   Ding dong, Jesus Christ is born!
   A precious child from heaven.
   Refrain

Glad Christmas Bells

Traditional English carol

Glad_ Christmas bells, your_ mu-sic tells, The_ sweet and pleasant sto—ry; How_ came to earth, in___ low-ly birth, The__ Lord of life and glo——ry.

2. No palace hall, its ceiling tall,
   His kingly head spread over,
   There only stood a stable rude
   The heav'nly babe to cover.

3. No raiment gay, as there He lay,
   Adorned the infant stranger;
   Poor, humble child of mother mild,
   She laid Him in a manger.

4. But from afar, a splendid star,
   The wise men westward turning;
   The livelong night, saw pure and bright,
   Above His birthplace burning.

I Heard the Bells on Christmas Day

Words by Henry Wadsworth Longfellow
(1807–1882)

Music by John Baptiste Calkin
(1827–1905)

1. I heard the bells on Christ-mas day Their old fa - mil - iar ca - rols play, And
2. I thought how, as the day had come, The bel-fries of all Christ-en-dom Had

wild and sweet the words re - peat Of peace on earth, good will to men.
roll'd a - long th'un - bro - ken song Of peace on earth, good will to men.

3. Till, ringing, swinging on its way,
The world revolved from night to day,
A voice, a chime, a chant sublime
Of peace on earth, good will to men.

4. Then from each black, accursèd mouth
The cannon thundered in the South,
And with the sound, the carols drowned
Of peace on earth, good will to men.

5. It was as if an earthquake rent
The hearth-stones of a continent,
And made forlorn the households born
Of peace on earth, good will to men.

6. And in despair I bowed my head;
"There is no peace on earth," I said;
"For hate is strong, and mocks the song
Of peace on earth, good will to men."

7. Then pealed the bells more loud and deep:
"God is not dead; nor doth He sleep!
The wrong shall fail, the right prevail,
With peace on earth, good will to men."

He Is Born
(Il est né)

Traditional French carol

2. *Ah! qu'il est beau, qu'il est charmant,*
   Ah! que ses grâces son parfaites.
   Ah! qu'il est beau, qu'il est charmant,
   Qu'il est doux ce divin enfant.
       Refrain

3. *Une étable est son logement,*
   Un peu de paille est sa couchette,
   Une étable est son logement,
   Pour un Dieu, quel abaissement.
       Refrain

4. *O Jésus, ô roi tout poissant,*
   Tout petit enfant que vous etes,
   O Jésus, ô roi tout poissant,
   Régnez sur nous entièrement.
       Refrain

Pat-a-pan

Traditional French carol

1. Willie, bring your little drum; Robin, bring your fife and come; And be merry while you play, Tu-re-lu-re-lu, Pat-a-pat-a pan, Come be merry while you play, Let us make our Christmas gay!

2. When the men of olden days
   To the King of kings gave praise,
   On the fife and drum did play,
     Tu-re-lu-re-lu,
     Pat-a-pat-a-pan,
   On the fife and drum did play,
   So their hearts were glad and gay!

3. God and man today become
   More in tune than fife and drum,
   So be merry while you play,
     Tu-re-lu-re-lu,
     Pat-a-pat-a-pan,
   So be merry while you play,
   Sing and dance this Christmas Day!

Christmas Chimes

Words and music by Henry Brinley Richards
(1817–1885)

What bells are those, so soft and clear, That fall me-lo-dious on mine ear?

Say, moth-er say,__ the whole night long, E'en in my dreams I heard their song, And

walk-ing in the morn-ing time, A-gain I heard their joy-ous chime.

What bells are these? say, Moth-er, say! What bells are those? say, Moth-er, say! My

child, they glo - rious ti - dings bring, Those bells their Christ-mas car-ol sing, Oh,

joy to us, ___ A Child is born, ___ A Son ___ is giv'n, Hail Christ-mas morn! The

Star - ry Hosts that line the sky, Sing glo-ry to God, to God on High;

Glo - ry to God on Earth be Peace, To men Sal - va - tion and re - lease.

Chorus

Glo - ry to God! hark! hark! the strain mounts up from yon - der hoa - ry fane, And ris - ing with me - lo - dious voice, Bids high and low to - day re - joice, Bids high and low to - day re - joice. Glo - ry to God! hark! hark! the strain, Glo - ry to God, on earth be Peace.

O Christmas Tree

Traditional German carol

Moderately

1. O Christ-mas tree, O Christ-mas tree, How true you stand un - chang - ing. O

Christ-mas tree, O Christ-mas tree, How true you stand un - chang - ing. Your

boughs so green in sum-mer-time, Re - main so green in win-ter-time. O

Christ-mas tree, O Christ-mas tree, How true you stand un - chang - ing.

2. O Christmas tree, O Christmas tree,
Thy message is enduring;
O Christmas tree, O Christmas tree,
Thy message is enduring.
So long ago in Bethlehem
Was born the Savior of all men;
O Christmas tree, O Christmas tree,
Thy message is enduring.

3. O Christmas tree, O Christmas tree,
Thy faith remains unchanging;
O Christmas tree, O Christmas tree,
Thy faith remains unchanging.
A symbol sent from God above,
Proclaiming Him the Lord of Love;
O Christmas tree, O Christmas tree,
Thy faith remains unchanging!

Deck the Hall

Traditional Welsh carol

Lively

1. { Deck the hall with boughs of hol-ly,
Fa la la la la la la la la.
'Tis the sea-son to be jol-ly,
Fa la la la la la la la la.

Don we now our gay ap-par-el,
Fa la la la la la la la la.

Troll the an-cient Yule-tide car-ol,
Fa la la la la la la la la.

2. See the blazing Yule before us,
Fa-la-la-la-la, la-la-la-la.
Strike the harp and join the chorus,
Fa-la-la-la-la, la-la-la-la.
Follow me in merry measure,
Fa-la-la, la-la-la, la-la-la.
While I tell of Yuletide treasure,
Fa-la-la-la-la, la-la-la-la.

3. Fast away the old year passes,
Fa-la-la-la-la, la-la-la-la.
Hail the new, ye lads and lasses,
Fa-la-la-la-la, la-la-la-la.
Sing we joyous all together,
Fa-la-la, la-la-la, la-la-la.
Heedless of the wind and weather,
Fa-la-la-la-la, la-la-la-la.

The Holly and the Ivy

Traditional English carol

1. The hol-ly and the i-vy, When they are both full grown, Of all the trees that are in the wood The hol-ly bears the crown.

2. The hol-ly bears a blos-som As white as lil-y flow'r, And Mar-y bore sweet Je-sus Christ To be our sweet Sav-ior.

Refrain

The ris-ing of the sun And the run-ning of the deer, The play-ing of the mer-ry or-gan, Sweet sing-ing in the choir.

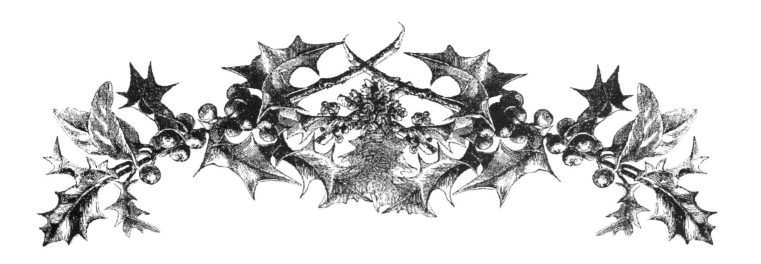

3. The holly bears a berry
   As red as any blood,
   And Mary bore sweet Jesus Christ
   To do poor sinners good.
   Refrain

4. The holly bears a prickle
   As sharp as any thorn,
   And Mary bore sweet Jesus Christ
   On Christmas Day in the morn.
   Refrain

5. The holly bears a bark
   As bitter as any gall,
   And Mary bore sweet Jesus Christ
   For to redeem us all.
   Refrain

6. The holly and the ivy,
   Now both are full well grown,
   Of all the trees that are in the wood
   The holly bears the crown.
   Refrain

Christ Was Born on Christmas Day

Words by John M. Neale
(1818–1866)

Traditional German carol

2. He is born to set us free,
   He is born our Lord to be:
   Ex Maria Virgine,
   The God, the Lord, by all adored forever

3. Let the bright red berries glow
   Everywhere in goodly show:
   Christus natus hodie,
   The Babe, the Son, the Holy One of Mary.

4. Christian men, rejoice and sing
   'Tis the birthday of a king:
   Ex Maria Virgine,
   The God, the Lord, by all adored forever.

Gather Around the Christmas Tree

Words and music by John Henry Hopkins
(1820–1891)

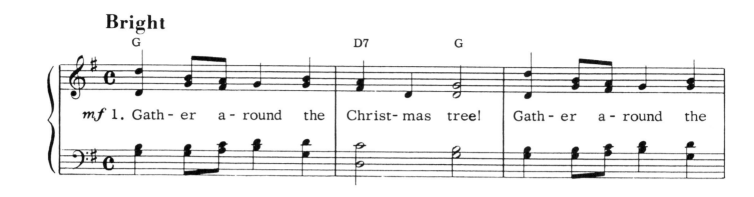

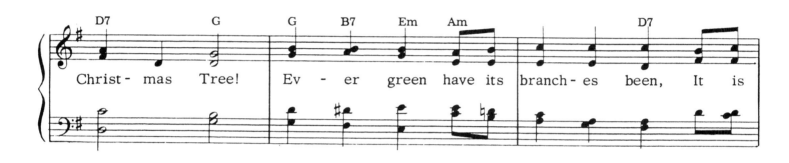

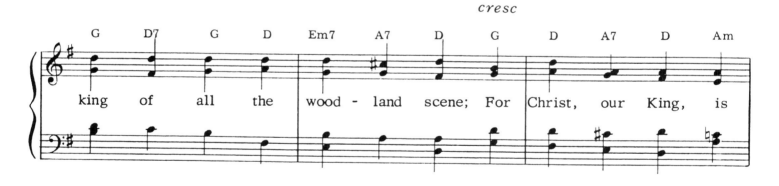

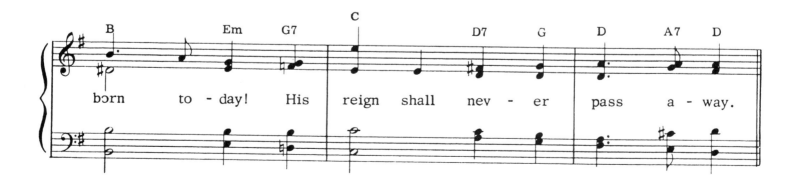

REFRAIN

Ho - san - na, Ho - san - na, Ho - san - na in the high - est.

2. Gather around the Christmas tree!
   Gather around the Christmas tree!
   Once the pride of the mountainside,
   Now cut down to grace our Christmastide:
   For Christ from heav'n to earth come down,
   To gain, through death, a noble crown.
   Refrain

3. Gather around the Christmas tree!
   Gather around the Christmas tree!
   Ev'ry bough bears a burden now,
   They are gifts of love for us, we trow:
   For Christ is born, His love to show,
   And give good gifts to me below.
   Refrain

Lo, How a Rose E'er Blooming

Traditional German carol

The Cherry Tree Carol

Traditional English carol

2. When Joseph and Mary walked through an orchard green,
   There were berries and cherries as thick as might be seen,
   There were berries and cherries as thick as might be seen.

3. And Mary spoke to Joseph, so meek and so mild:
   "Joseph, gather me some cherries for I am with child,"
   "Joseph, gather me some cherries for I am with child."

4. And Joseph flew in anger, in anger flew he:
   "Let the father of the baby gather cherries for thee,"
   "Let the father of the baby gather cherries for thee."

5. The up spoke baby Jesus from in Mary's womb:
   "Bend down the tallest tree that my mother might have some,"
   "Bend down the tallest tree that my mother might have some."

6. And bent down the tallest branch till it touchèd Mary's hand,
   Cried she, "Oh, look thou Joseph, I have cherries by command."
   Cried she, "Oh, look thou Joseph, I have cherries by command."

Here We Come A-Wassailing

Traditional English carol

3. We are not daily beggars
   That beg from door to door,
   But we are neighbors' children
   Whom you have seen before:
   Refrain

4. Call up the butler of this house
   Put on his golden ring;
   Let him bring us up a glass of beer
   And better we shall sing:
   Refrain

5. We have got a little purse
   Of stretching leather skin;
   We want a little of your money
   To line it well within:
   Refrain

6. Bring us out a table
   And spread it with a cloth;
   Bring us out a mouldy cheese
   And some of your Christmas loaf;
   Refrain

7. God bless the master of this house
   God bless the mistress too;
   And all the little children
   That round the table go:
   Refrain

8. Good master and good mistress
   While you're sitting by the fire,
   Pray think of us poor children
   Who are wandering in the mire:
   Refrain

The·Boar's·Head·

The·Wassail·Bowl·

The Gloucester Wassail

Traditional English carol

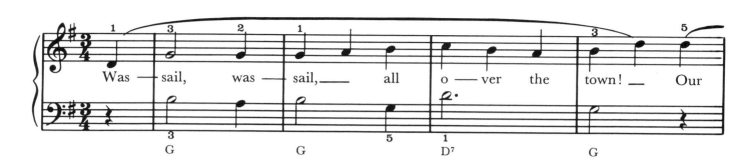

Was — sail, was — sail,___ all o — ver the town! ___ Our

bread it is white, and our ale ___ it ___ is brown, Our

bowl ___ it ___ is ___ made of the white ma — ple tree; With the

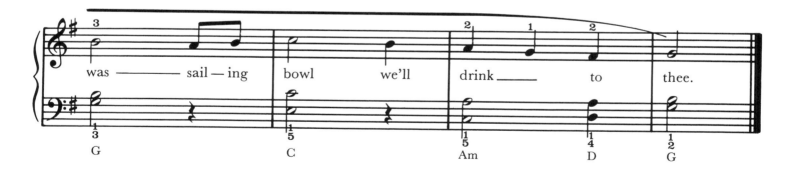

was ———— sail—ing bowl we'll drink___ to thee.

Dame Get Up and Bake Your Pies

Traditional English song

Dame, get up ___ and bake your pies,
Bake your pies, bake your pies,
Dame, get up ___ and bake your pies On
Christ ___ mas Day in the morn ___ ing.

Gm Cm⁶ D Gm D⁷ Gm Cm⁶ D Gm D⁷ Gm

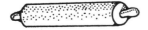

Masters in This Hall

Words by William Morris
(1834–1896)

Traditional French tune

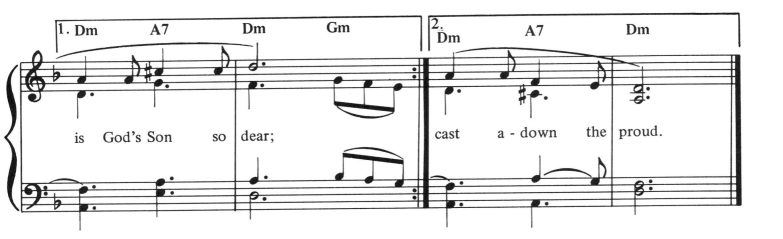

is God's Son so dear;

cast a-down the proud.

2. Then to Bethl'em town
   We went two and two;
   In a sorry place
   We heard the oxen low:
   Refrain

3. Ox and ass Him know,
   Kneeling on their knee,
   Wond'rous joy had I
   This little babe to see:
   Refrain

Christmas Is Coming

Traditional English round

Christ - mas is com - ing! The goose is get - ting fat;

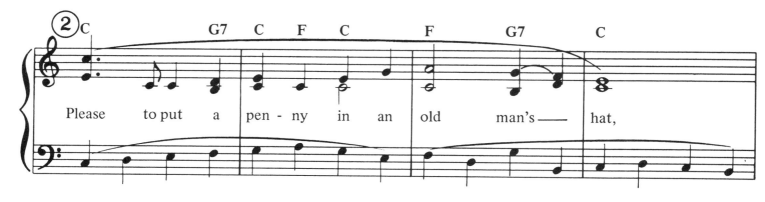

Please to put a pen - ny in an old man's —— hat,

Please to put a pen - ny in an old man's —— hat.

If you have no penny,
A ha'penny will do,
If you have no ha'penny
Then God bless you,
If you have no ha'penny
Then God bless you.

The Boar's Head Carol

Traditional English carol

2. The boar's head as I understand
   Is the bravest dish in all the land,
   When thus bedecked with a gay garland
   Let us *servire cantico*.
   (Let us now serve it with a song.)
       Refrain

3. Our steward hath provided this
   In honor of the King of Bliss,
   Which on this day to be servèd is,
   In reginensi atrio.
   (All within this royal hall.)
       Refrain

Jacques Come Here

Traditional French carol

Moderate

Jacques, come here, Bring - ing cheer, why so sad, pray

tell, May our song ring out strong as we sing No - el!

Mar - got can sing _____ the high notes all a - lone,

Pier - rot can sing _____ the ten - or part you see,

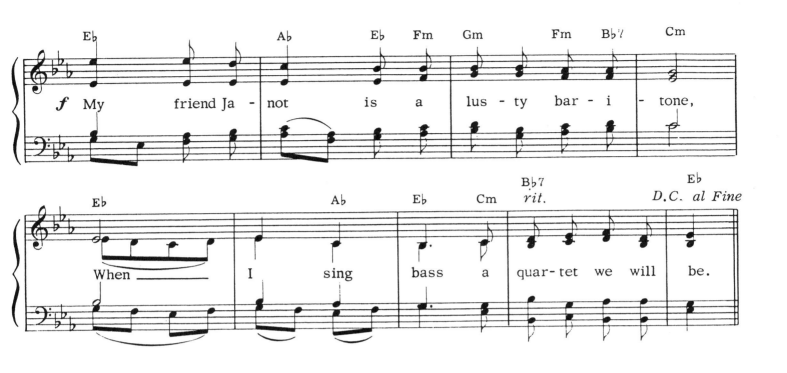

f My friend Ja - not is a lus - ty bar - i - tone,

When _____ I sing bass a quar - tet we will be.

We Wish You a Merry Christmas

Traditional English carol

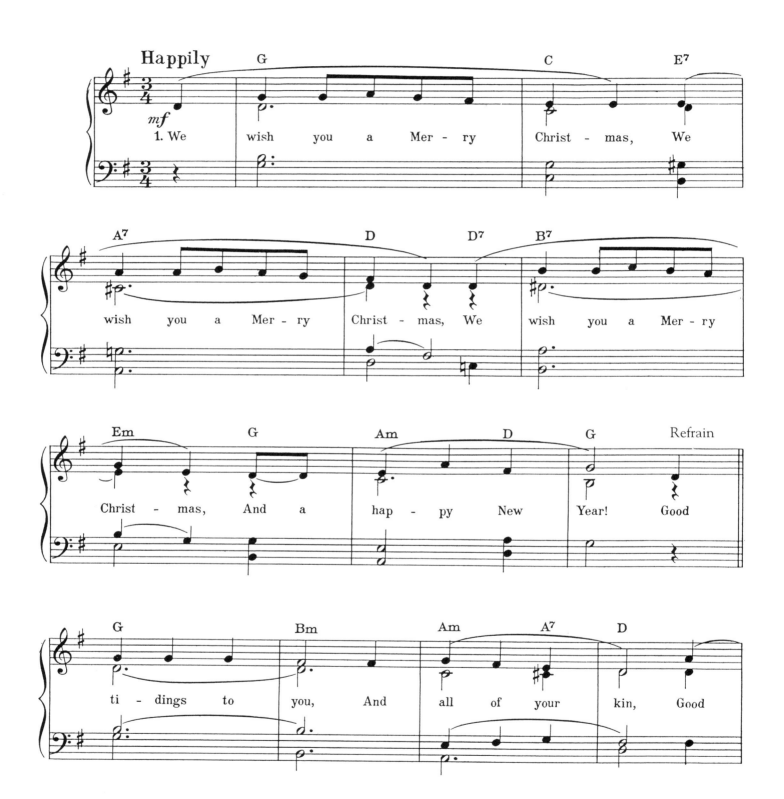

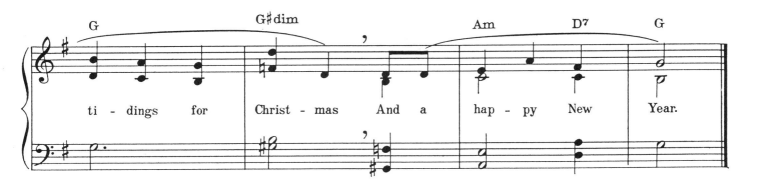

G♯dim   Am   D7   G

ti - dings for Christ - mas And a hap - py New Year.

2. Oh, bring us some figgy pudding,
Oh, bring us some figgy pudding,
Oh, bring us some figgy pudding,
And bring it right here!
Refrain

3. We won't go until we get some,
We won't go until we get some,
We won't go until we get some,
So bring it right here.
Refrain

4. For we all like figgy pudding,
We all like figgy pudding,
We all like figgy pudding,
So bring it right here.
Refrain

The Twelve Days of Christmas

Traditional English carol

G7 **C** **F** **B♭** **F** **C7** **F** **B♭** **F**

Two— tur - tle doves, and a par - tridge— in a pear tree.

F **Dm** **C** **F** **C** **Gm7**

6. On the sixth day of Christ - mas my | true love gave to me | Six geese a - lay - ing,
7. On the seventh day of Christ - mas my | true love gave to me | Sev - en swans a - swim - ming,
8. On the eighth day of Christ - mas my | true love gave to me | Eight maids a - milk - ing,
9. On the ninth day of Christ - mas my | true love gave to me | Nine la - dies wait - ing,
10. On the tenth day of Christ - mas my | true love gave to me | Ten lords a - leap - ing,
11. On the eleventh day of Christ - mas my | true love gave to me | 'Lev - en pip - ers pip - ing,
12. On the twelfth day of Christ - mas my | true love gave to me | Twelve drum - mers drum - ming,

Am Dm G7 **C** **F** **Dm** **Gm** **Dm**

Five gold - en rings, Four— call - ing birds, Three French hens,

G7 **C** **F** **B♭** **F** **C7** **6,7,8,9,10,11.** **F B♭ F** **12.** **F B♭ F**

Two— tur - tle doves, and a par - tridge— in a pear tree. tree.

D.S. *rit.*

* *Repeat this measure as often as necessary to sing the accumulated lyrics of all previous verses, each time ending with "Six geese a-laying."*

Auld Lang Syne

Words by Robert Burns
(1759–1796)

Traditional Scottish air

Good King Wenceslas

Words by John M. Neale
(1818–1866)

Traditional Swedish melody

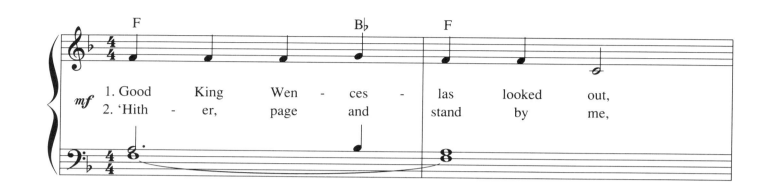

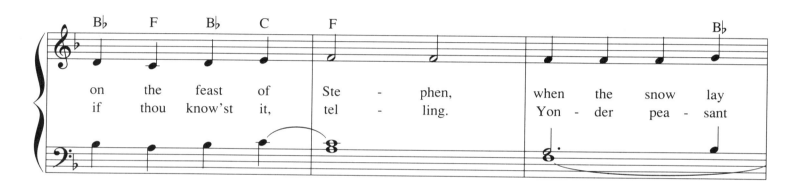

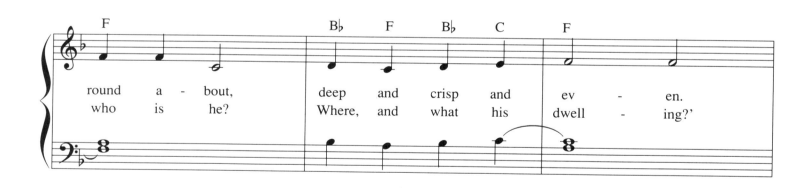

cru - el,
moun - tain.

when a poor man
Right a - gainst the

came in sight,
for - est fence,

gath - 'ring win - ter
by St. Ag - nes

fu -
foun -

el.
tain.

3. "Bring me flesh, and bring me wine,
Bring me pinelogs hither;
Thou and I shall see him dine
When we bear them thither."
Page and monarch forth they went,
Forth they went together:
Through the rude wind's wild lament
And the bitter weather.

4. "Sire, the night is darker now,
And the wind blows stronger;
Fails my heart, I know not how,
I can go no longer."
"Mark my footsteps good, my page;
Tread thou in them boldly.
Thou shalt find the winter's rage
Freeze thy blood less coldly."

5. In his master's steps he trod,
Where the snow lay dinted;
Heat was in the very sod
Which the saint had printed.
Therefore, Christian men be sure,
Wealth or rank possesing,
Ye who now will bless the poor,
Shall youselves find blessing.

Old Welsh New Year's Song

Traditional Welsh song

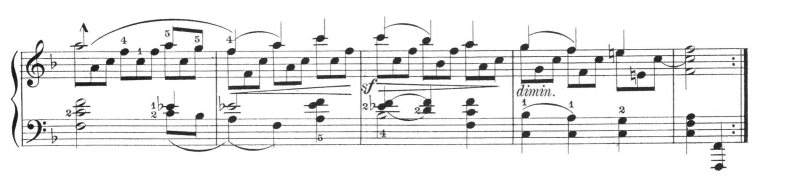

Christmas Classics

The Star of Bethlehem

F.E. Weatherly

Stephen Adams
(1844–1913)

rall.

heard the church bells ring - ing, I saw the bright stars shine, And

child - hood came a - gain to me, With all its dreams di - vine.

a tempo

Then, as I lis t'ned to the bells, And watch'd the skies a - far,

Out of the East ma - jes - ti - cal There rose one ra - diant star; And

From street to street it led me, by man-y a man-sion fair, It

shone thro' din-gy case-ment on man-y a gar-ret bare; From high-way on to high-way, thro'

al - leys dark and cold, And where it shone the dark-ness was

flood - ed all with gold. Sad hearts for-got their sor - row, Rough

hearts grew soft and mild, And wea-ry lit-tle chil - dren

turn'd in their sleep and smil'd; While man-y a home-less wan - der-er up -

lift - ed pa-tient eyes _____ Seem - ing to see a

home at last be-yond those star-ry skies.

Seem-ing to see a home at last be yond those star - ry

skies.

And then me-thought earth

fad - ed, I rose as borne on wings, Be -

Tempo I.

then the gates roll'd back — — ward, I

stood where An - gels trod; It was the star, the star of

dim. *grandioso*

Beth-le-hem had led me up to God, The star, the

ad lib.

star, had led me up to God.

colla voce *simile*

Jesu, Joy of Man's Desiring

Johann Sebastian Bach
(1685–1750)

wis - dom, Love___ most bright,
un - cre - a - ted light.

Word of God, our flesh___ that fash - ioned

throne.

rit.

Prepare Thyself, Zion

from *Christmas Oratorio*

Johann Sebastian Bach
(1685–1750)

Christmas Song

César Franck
(1822–1890)

Allegretto

The Christmas Tree

Niels Gade
(1817–1890)

Ring Out, Wild Bells

Alfred, Lord Tennyson
(1809–1892)

Charles Gounod
(1818–1893)

Jesus of Nazareth

Charles Gounod
(1818–1893)

robe roy - al en - fold Him; Your King de -
jet - tent la pier - - re, sur vo - tre

scends to earth from bright - er home.____
cœur a - - vez - vous mis la main?

Tho' poor be the cham - ber, come here, come and a - dore;____
Né dans u - ne crê - che, di - vin Ré - demp - teur,____

Lo! the Lord of Heav - en hath to mor - tals giv - en
i - ci - bas_ je prê - che, i - ci - bas_ je prê - che

life__ for - ev - er - more._____
les__ ver - tus du cœur._____

Wind, to the ce - dars pro -
A - veu - gles nés,_____ mu -

claim the joy - ful sto - ry; Wave of the
ets, pa - ra - ly - ti - ques, pau - vres the per -

sea,_____ the ti - dings bear a - far._____ The
dus, boi - teux, sourds ap - pro - chez._____ Du

Hallelujah Chorus
from *Messiah*

George Frideric Handel
(1685–1759)

Allegretto moderato

He Shall Feed His Flock

from *Messiah*

George Frideric Handel
(1685–1759)

He shall gath - er the lambs with His arm, with _____ His arm,

and car - ry__ them in His bos - om, and

gent - ly lead those_ that are__ with young, and gent - ly_ lead,__ and

gent - ly lead those that are with young.   Come__

__ un-to Him, __ all ye that la - bor, come un - to Him, ye that

are heav-y la-den, and He will give you rest, Come

mf   *p*

un - to Him, __ all ye that la - bor, Come __ un-to Him, ye

that are heav-y la-den, and He will give you rest.

mf

Take His yoke up-on you, and learn of Him, for He __ is __ meek __ and

p

low - ly of heart,   and ye shall find rest, __ and ye shall find rest un-

to __ your souls,   Take His yoke up - on   you, and

learn of Him,   for He __ is __ meek __ and low - ly of heart, __   and

ye shall find __ rest, __   and ye shall find rest __ un - to __ your souls.

I Know That My Redeemer Liveth

from *Messiah*

George Frideric Handel
(1685–1759)

day _____ up-on the earth.

I know that my Re-deem-er liv-eth, and that He shall stand _____

_____ at the lat - ter day up-on the earth, _____ up-on the

earth. I know _____ that my Re-deem - er liv-eth, and that He shall stand at the

lat - - ter day up-on the earth, _____ up-on the _ earth:

And though worms de-stroy this bod-y,

yet in my flesh shall I see God, yet in my flesh shall I see God.

I know that my Re - deem - er liv - eth,

them that sleep, the first — fruits of them — that sleep.

For now is Christ ris - en, for now is Christ

ris - en from the dead, the first — fruits

Adagio

of them that sleep.

cresc.

A Sleigh Ride

Richard Kleinmichel
(1846–1901)

Allegro non troppo

March of the Toys

from *Babes in Toyland*

John Alan Haughton

Victor Herbert
(1859–1924)

Toyland

from *Babes in Toyland*

Victor Herbert
(1859–1924)

Very Slow

... When

you're grown up, my dears ___ And are as old as I ___ You'll oft - en pon - der

on the years That roll so swift - ly by, my dears, that roll so swift - ly by ___ And

of the man - y lands ___ You will have jour-neyed through ___ You'll oft re - call The

best of all, The land your child-hood knew! ___ Your child - hood knew.

Chorus
Tempo I

Toy - land! Toy - land! Lit - tle girl and boy - land, while you dwell with-

in it ___ You are ev - er hap-py then. Child - hood's Joy - land, Mys-tic mer - ry

Toy - land! Once you pass - its bor-ders you can ne'er re-turn a - gain.

Ring Out, Wild Bells

Alfred, Lord Tennyson
(1809–1892)

Wolfgang Amadeus Mozart
(1756–1791)

2. Ring out the old, ring in the new,
   Ring, happy bells, across the snow:
   The year is going, let him go;
   Ring out the false, ring in the true.

3. Ring out false pride in place and blood,
   The civic slander and the spite;
   Ring in the love of truth and right,
   Ring in the common love of good.

4. Ring in the valiant man and free,
   The larger heart, the kindlier hand;
   Ring out the darkness of the land,
   Ring in the Christ that is to be.

Alleluia

Wolfgang Amadeus Mozart
(1756–1791)

Allegro

f Al - le - lu - ja, al - le - lu - ja,____ Al - le -
lu - ja, al - le - lu - ja! Al - le - lu - ja, al -
le - lu - ja,____ Al - le - lu - ja, al - le - lu -
ja! Al - le - lu - ja,

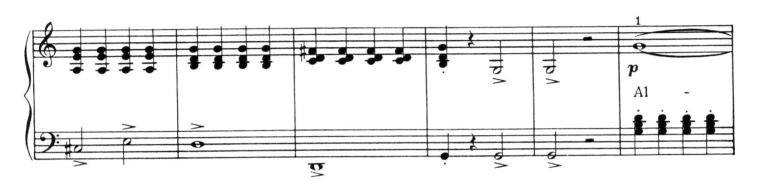

le - lu - ja

Al - le - lu - ja, al -

le - lu - ja! Al - le - lu - ja,

al - le - lu - ja, al - le -

lu - ja, al - le -

lu - ja! *f* *ff*

March of the Tin Soldiers

from *The Nutcracker*

Peter Ilyich Tchaikovsky
(1840–1893)

Dance of the Sugar Plum Fairy

from *The Nutcracker*

Peter Ilyich Tchaikovsky
(1840–1893)

Dance of the Mirlitons

from *The Nutcracker*

Peter Ilyich Tchaikovsky
(1840–1893)

Waltz of the Flowers

from *The Nutcracker*

Peter Ilyich Tchaikovsky
(1840–1893)

Tempo di valse

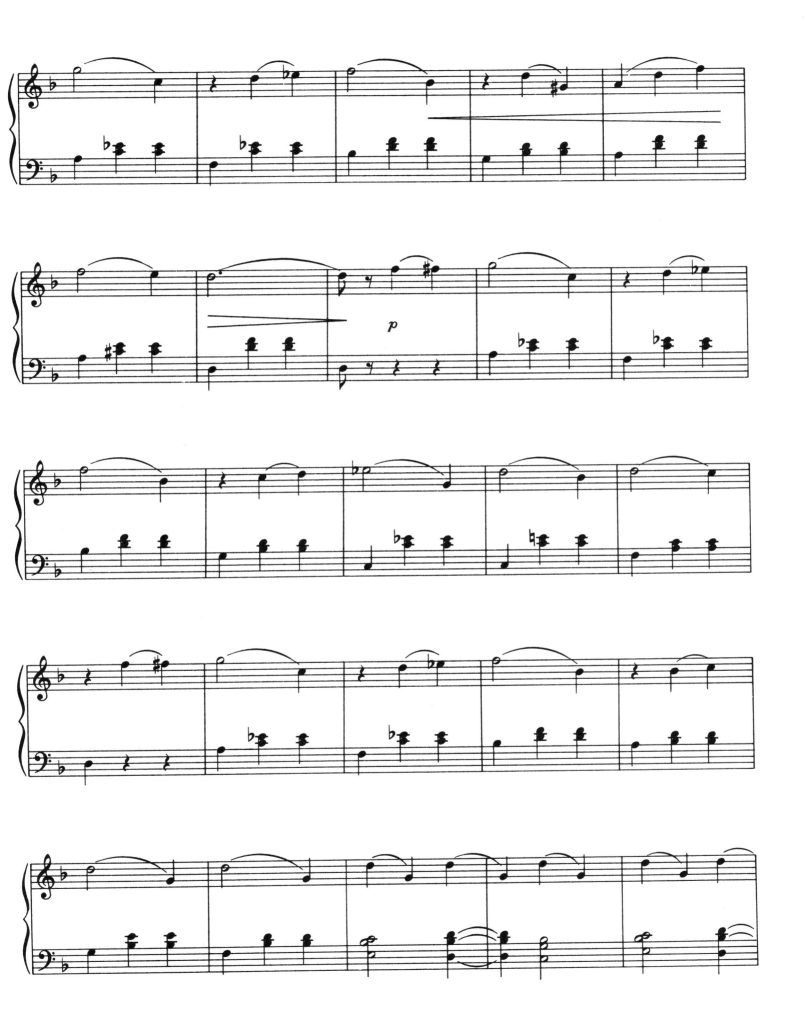

Russian Dance

from *The Nutcracker*

Peter Ilyich Tchaikovsky
(1840–1893)

Skaters Waltz

Emil Waldteufel
(1837–1915)

Index